SO-CEX-779

Holidays Are Holy Days

Sermons For Special Sundays

Alex A. Gondola, Jr.

CSS Publishing Company, Inc., Lima, Ohio

HOLIDAYS ARE HOLY DAYS

Library of Congress Cataloging-in-Publication Data

Gondola, Alex A.
  Holidays are holy days : sermons for special Sundays / Alex A. Gondola, Jr.
      p. cm.
  ISBN 0-7880-2328-4 (perfect bound : alk paper)
  1. Church year sermons. 2. Sermons, American. I. Title.

BV0.G618 2004
252'.6—dc22

2004013862

For more information about CSS Publishing Company resources, visit our website at www.csspub.com or e-mail us at custserv@csspub.com or call (800) 241-4056.

Dedicated to
the members and friends of
Dennis Union Church
(United Church of Christ)
who helped make my
holidays holy days
for ten years

Acknowledgments

This is the fourth book I have written in five years. The completion of these books is less a personal accomplishment than it is a tribute to the encouragement, support — and toleration — I have received from many people around me. The members and friends of Dennis Union Church (UCC) of Dennis, Massachusetts, have welcomed these sermons. The church leadership graciously gave me the opportunity to write. I was blessed with outstanding colleagues and co-workers at Dennis Union Church: The Rev. Dr. Constance S. Bickford, The Rev. William W. Tucker, Mary Lou Earle, Ruth Giger, Steve Lovejoy, Jane Springer, Noel Tipton, and Barbara Wells. Nancy McKiernan, DUC Church Office Administrator, was particularly helpful in assembling this collection. My wife Bonnie, as always, is a supportive and insightful reader. Our son Andrew continues to keep our lives interesting. It has been a privilege to work again with CSS Publishing Company and with editors Teresa Rhoads, Becky Brandt, and Stan Purdum. I'm also grateful to the writers, preachers, professors, clergy colleagues, retreat and seminar leaders, church members, and other sources that inspired or influenced these sermons. This collection was assembled from more than 25 years of preaching to four different congregations. I've tried very hard to acknowledge every source. Some may inadvertently have been overlooked or lost over the years. If so, I beg their pardon and sincerely thank them as well.

Table Of Contents

Preface   11

New Year's Day
It's About Time   13
   Galatians 4:4-7
New Beginnings For A New Year   19
   1 Corinthians 11:23-26

Martin Luther King, Jr., Day
Called, Commissioned, And Comforted:
A Tribute To Dr. Martin Luther King, Jr.   25
   Isaiah 49:1-9
Privilege And Prejudice   31
   1 Corinthians 12:7-13

Super Bowl Sunday
Going For The Goal In Football And Faith   37
   Hebrews 12:1-3, 12a

Valentine's Day
Valentines   43
   1 Corinthians 12:31b—13:8a, 13

Presidents' Day
First In War, First In Peace   49
   Psalm 1
The Faith Of Abraham   55
   Hebrews 11:1, 8-16

Saint Patrick's Day
Christ In All Things: The Faith Of Saint Patrick   61
   Romans 5:1-5

April Fool's Day
Where Are The Clowns? 67
  1 Corinthians 1:26-31
The Feast Of Fools 71
  1 Corinthians 1:18-31

Earth Day
(He) Put The Whole World In Our Hands 75
  Psalm 8; Proverbs 8:1-4, 22-31
Theology And Ecology For A Small Planet 81
  Psalm 8; Genesis 1:26-31

Mother's Day
Anger 87
  Ephesians 4:25-32; Matthew 5:21-24
The Motherhood Of God 93
  Isaiah 66:10-14a; Hosea 11:1-4; Matthew 23:37-39

Memorial Day
Memorial Daze 99
  Ecclesiasticus 44:1-15
Good Grief 105
  John 11:17-36

Father's Day
Help Wanted: Fathers 111
  Ephesians 6:1-4; 1 Corinthians 13:4-8a
The Parable Of The Prodigal Parent 115
  Luke 15:11-24

Fourth Of July
Our Two Flags 121
  Romans 13:1-7
America The Beautiful 127
  Matthew 22:15-22

Labor Day
Is Work A Four-Letter Word?   131
  Psalm 104; Genesis 1:1-5, 31
Don't Just Do Something, Sit There!   137
  Luke 10:38-42

Grandparent's Day (Second Sunday Of September)
What's So Grand About Grandparents?   143
  1 Corinthians 13

Columbus Day/Indigenous Peoples' Day
Good-bye, Columbus?   149
  Psalm 19:4; Isaiah 61:1-3
Indian Givers   155
  Psalm 95:1-7a

Halloween/All Saints' Day/Reformation Sunday
We Need A Good Priest — Always   161
  Hebrews 7:23-28
I Love Luther   167
  Romans 1:8-17

Veterans' Day
One Nation, Under God   173
  Joshua 24:1-3a, 14-25
The Greatest Generation   179
  Matthew 11:16-19

Thanksgiving
Don't Be A Turkey!   185
  Luke 17:11-19
To Be A Pilgrim   191
  Hebrews 11:1-3, 13-16

Christmas
Don't Forget The Child!   197
  Micah 5:2-5a; Luke 1:46-55
A Christmas That Lasts   203
  Luke 2:1-20

Preface

"Did you preach on the Veterans on Memorial Day weekend?" an older relative used to ask me when I first began preaching. He was a World War II veteran himself, and proud of it. He was disappointed if I told him that on that Memorial Day Sunday I hadn't preached on the Veterans. "You should," he would say. "That's what Memorial Day is about." This interchange illustrates a preacher's dilemma. Almost every month has a secular holiday in it. Some months have several. Parishioners frequently have expectations about what they will hear in worship on those Sundays. They may come to church primed for a paean on motherly love on Mother's Day or a rousing patriotic sermon around the Fourth of July or a tribute to Pilgrim piety on Thanksgiving Sunday. I quickly discovered ignoring these holidays completely has its perils. (As a student minister I once scheduled a youth fellowship activity for Mother's Day afternoon — to howls of protest from teenagers and parents.) On those Sundays close to a national holiday it's the preacher's challenge to try to distinguish between civil religion and the Christian religion and to attempt to speak the Word with integrity, usually while making some acknowledgment of the holiday.

This challenge is also an opportunity. Our English word "holiday" originally derived from the words "holy" and "day." Holidays were meant to be "holy days." This volume reflects my efforts over a quarter century plus of preaching to view civic celebrations in the light of faith. Hopefully this collection will encourage other preachers to bring their own insights to bear on holiday preaching. It might aid the lay reader to consider these holidays from a new perspective. With creativity and the blessing of the Holy Spirit, our holidays can be holy days again.

It's About Time

Galatians 4:4-7

One of the gifts my wife Bonnie and I gave each other this Christmas is an antique clock. It's a gingerbread style clock about a hundred years old. It has a handsome oak case with elaborate carving and delicate gold maple leaves painted on the etched glass plate across the front. Its pendulum ticks off the seconds. The clock chimes the hours and half-hours. It's charming and quite different from the digital clocks in the house. It was fun to learn about the old clock's history, how to set it up, wind it, and adjust it.

But the clock wasn't a delight in the middle of the night a couple of nights later. That night I woke around 2 a.m. and couldn't get back to sleep no matter what I tried. Finally, I climbed out of bed and stumbled to our living room as I sometimes do to sit in a comfortable chair to try to get sleepy again. But from about 2:30 to 3:30 the tick-tock of the clock, so charming in daylight, seemed loud and annoying in the dark. It reminded me I was still awake. It reminded me the night was passing. Chiming on the half-hour and hour only rubbed it in.

The old clock was reminding me time has two faces. As Paul Tillich puts it, "Time is our hope" and "Time is our despair." Time well spent is a joy and delight, just as the old clock was a joy and delight to us the day that we purchased it. But the passage of time can also lead to despair. Each ticking second and ringing hour brings us closer to dying. Tillich again: "The voice of the clock has reminded many people of the fact that they are timed." We don't so much have time as time has us. For, as the old hymn puts it, "Time like an ever-rolling stream bears all who breathe away; we fly, forgotten as a dream dies at the opening day."

This is the first Sunday of a New Year. Around this time, time may be on our minds. We may look back over the past year. We may look forward to the future. This time of year especially we are sensitive to what Tillich called "the mystery of time."[1] This caused me to wonder, "What does scripture have to say about time? And what awareness of time might we bring to the New Year?"

Ancient Greek, the language of the Christian scriptures, the New Testament, is in some ways more precise than English. For example, in English we have only one word for time: "time." The Greeks had at least two. *Chronos* was *quantitative* time, time that can be measured, chronological hours, minutes, and seconds. *Chronos* is the time the clock ticks off. It's what we refer to when we say, "Remember to get to your appointment on time." Or wonder, "How much longer can this sermon go on?"

Kairos, on the other hand, was *qualitative* time. *Kairos* was used about 85 times in the Bible. It means "quality time" or "the right time" or "the opportune moment." *Kairos* moments are the time to act, to "seize the day," "strike while the iron is hot," "grab the brass ring," or "go for the gold," to use common English expressions. God willing, we will have both *chronos* time and *kairos* time in the year ahead. As we enter into a New Year, can we keep in mind these two aspects of time?

On the one hand, let's be aware that time (*chronos* time) is running out for us. Imagine, for example, you have a bank account with a balance of $86,400. Nice thought, isn't it! Only that $86,400 is only available to you for one day. At the end of that day, it's "use it or lose it." What would you do with the money? Draw it out and put it in an account that's more secure? What if that wasn't possible?

I'd want to spend the whole $86,400, hopefully wisely. I think I'd give a lot of it to worthy causes — although there are a few things I'd like for myself. Well, we all have an account like that. It's called TIME. Every morning we are credited with 86,400 seconds. By the end of the day every one of them is spent. We will never get them back. The beginning of a New Year is a good time for a resolution to strive to use our time well.

Let's not wait until it's too late to do the things that are important. An insurance agent once received a phone call from a very excited woman. "I want to insure my house," she said, "can I do it over the phone?" The agent explained he'd have to go out and look over the property first. "Okay," she said, "but you'd better hurry up. It's on fire."

Time is precious. We need to spend it wisely, on things that matter, before it's too late. I once read an illustration about how our time can be filled. Imagine a large wooden chest with a dozen bowling balls in it. No more bowling balls can fit in. But there is still plenty of room between the bowling balls for marbles. Even when as many marbles as possible are packed in, there would still be spaces between the marbles for sand. Even if the box were filled with bowling balls, marbles, and sand, we could still pour in buckets of water. Just as that wooden chest could be filled with ever-smaller particles, so also we can make good use of ever-smaller amounts of time.

The late Arthur Michael Ramsey, a busy man, the former Archbishop of Canterbury, was once asked when he found time to write his books. He replied, "Monday, a quarter of an hour; Tuesday, ten minutes; Wednesday rather better, half an hour; Thursday not very good, but ten minutes; Friday, a bit of a lull, half an hour; Saturday, half an hour." Ramsey wrote a dozen significant books by making use of snippets of time.

In the year ahead, what could we do in our spare time, waiting for our computer to "boot up," waiting to get "on line," waiting on the phone on hold, waiting in the dentist's office, waiting for an oil change? Some folks carry around a prayer list and use those odd moments to pray for others. One retired pastor I know tries to memorize or review one Psalm daily. We could easily read through all four gospels in odd moments of time (when I read scripture, I like to read it aloud). We could carry around little cards and write out notes to cheer up shut-ins, compose poetry, or learn a foreign language. Time is fleeting. It's irretrievable. Every moment is precious. Therefore, as Ephesians 5:16 puts it, let us make the most of the time.

But then there is that second Greek understanding of time, *kairos* time, "quality time," "the right time" or "the opportune moment." In *kairos* time, even the seemingly insignificant can reveal God. For the great God who is above all time and beyond all time

15

chooses to meet us *in* time. Christianity is a historical religion. At its center is the proclamation that "the Word became flesh and dwelt among us" (John 1:14a RSV). God became a man. The eternal breaks into time.

Two thousand years ago, the Son of God was born in occupied Palestine of a peasant woman named Mary. He worked as a carpenter in a village in Galilee much of his life. But Jesus of Nazareth, a historical person, was also Jesus the Christ, "Emmanuel," God with us. As Paul puts it, "When the time had fully come, God sent forth his son, born of woman, born under the law" to redeem us (Galatians 4:7 RSV). At the right time, in God's time, God broke into history to redeem time.

"The time is fulfilled, and the kingdom (or realm) of God is at hand," said Jesus (Mark 1:14b RSV). He meant God is near. God is here. God is "close at hand." God is as close at hand as this hymnal is in my hand right now. God is as close as the person sitting nearest to you in the pew — even closer. *That's* how close God is at this moment, if we have eyes to see.

You and I could meet God at any instant. It helps, of course, to be open to encountering God. William Blake, the poet and mystic, was. In a well-known poem he encourages us

To see the World in a grain of sand,
And a Heaven in a wild flower,
Hold infinity in the palm of your hand,
And eternity in an hour.

Blake met God in flowers and sand, in the beauty and wonder of nature. Have you ever sensed God's presence while walking along the beach or working in your garden? Have you suddenly felt different, as if all your senses were sharper, as if in that instant you were more fully alive? When we are aware of God's presence, eternity breaks in and an ordinary moment becomes *kairos*. In the year ahead, can we look for God in the beauty and wonder of the natural world?

Something of the eternal may also break through in seemingly ordinary actions. In his poem, "In Memoriam M.K.H. 1911-1984,"

Irish poet Seamus Heany writes of peeling potatoes alongside his mother on a Sunday morning when he was a child. He vividly recalls the gleaming bucket of water, the little pleasant splashes as the potatoes dropped, her head bent toward his, their breathing in unison. Heany never felt closer to his mother than in that moment, peeling potatoes with her on a Sunday morning. It was something he remembered while his mother lay dying.

We never know when we might be making a memory. We never know when God might reveal God's Self in some seemingly ordinary thing. As someone put it, "It may seem like just a minute, but eternity can be in it." Anything might become *kairos*, for the simplest activities can disclose the living God.

That same God who breaks into time also calls us to obedience. *Kairos* time is the time to choose. The Danish philosopher Soren Kierkegaard said every moment is the now of decision. He was right. At all times we must choose for or against God.

Martin Luther King, Jr., wrote, "Time ... can be used either destructively or constructively. I am coming to feel that the people of ill will have used time much more effectively than have the people of good will ... We must use time creatively, and forever realize that the time is always ripe to do right."[2]

King was right. "Let us not grow weary in well doing" (Ephesians 6:9 RSV). For the time is always ripe to do right. Right here, right now is the time to commit ourselves to racial justice. Right here, right now, is the moment to fight homelessness and hunger in our community. Right here, right now, is the time to pray for peace and to commit ourselves to peacemaking. *Kairos* time includes a demand for decision. In God's name, we must seize the time and redeem the time.

It's about time for us to take time seriously. God created time and gave a measure of it to each of us as a gift. Our *chronos* time is limited. The clock is ticking. So let's not "kill time" in the year ahead. Rather let us strive to use even small scraps of time wisely, on things that really matter.

Let's especially be alert for eternity breaking into the present. If we are sensitive and spiritually alert, any moment might become *kairos*, "God drenched" time for us. Let's strive to look for

17

God even in the ordinary. Let us listen constantly for God's call to service. For the kingdom of God (the realm of God) is at hand in every moment. He who has ears, she who has ears, let them hear (Matthew 11:15).

1. Paul Tillich, *The Shaking Of The Foundation* (New York: Charles Scribner's Sons, 1948), pp. 34-37.

2. Martin Luther King, Jr., in an American Friends Service Committee booklet, 1963, p. 9.

New Beginnings For A New Year

1 Corinthians 11:23-26

This past week, millions of Americans took part in traditional New Year's Eve celebrations. More than half-a-million people packed into Times Square. They were there to enjoy the crowd and to watch a big apple slide down the side of the Allied Chemical building. Additional millions stayed up late to watch Dick Clark's "New Year's Rockin' Eve" on television. In private homes, restaurants, and bars grown men and women put on pointy little hats and honked little horns, threw confetti, and sang "Auld Lang Syne." Many ate too much or drank too much and woke up reaching for Alka-Seltzer or Pepto Bismol on New Year's Day. That's how Americans traditionally celebrate the start of a New Year. Almost every year I pause and wonder, "Why?"

What do we seem to be searching for from this particular holiday? Why do some celebrate so frantically on New Year's Eve? I believe we're exuberant on New Year's Eve because the start of a New Year holds out the promise of a new beginning. The old year, for many, may seem tarnished, filled with memories of slights given and slights received, harsh words exchanged or disappointments suffered. Some may drink quite a lot in an effort to forget it. But the New Year is as innocent and unspoiled as a newborn baby. We can tell ourselves, "This year I'll make resolutions and keep them. This year I'll get things right."

Perhaps what we're longing for is a "do over." When I was a child we played softball on a half-acre field near my house. The field wasn't designed to be a ball field. It was convenient but had its limitations. Sometimes a batter would hit the ball over a wire fence and down into a gully, putting it temporarily out of play. When that happened we'd yell, "Do over!" Another ball would be introduced and the play would be run again. In golf, a "do over" is

19

called a "Mulligan." Sometimes we may long for a "do over" in life.

This longing for a "do over," for new beginnings in a New Year appears in many cultures. In Korea, at the New Year, each person decides what bad habits they want to get rid of and what past misdeeds they want forgiven. They write these things on a kite and launch it. When the kite is high in the sky they cut the string and let it go. In China, they do a thorough housecleaning in the New Year to get rid of evil spirits. In Italy, they open their windows at midnight on New Year's Eve to throw out old crockery, ugly ornaments, and detested furniture, plus anything that reminds them of what they'd rather forget.

Sometimes we'd like a new beginning but may find ourselves stuck in a rut. We revisit the same old sins, bad habits, or poisonous thoughts again and again. I once read a good description of a rut on the internet. In America the distance between the two rails on a train track is exactly 4-feet 8.5-inches wide.

Why is it that width? Because that was the distance between train tracks in Great Britain, and the earliest American railroad builders came from Britain. The British had designed their railroads around pre-railroad trams. The early tramcars were built to be the same width as the horse-drawn wagons that came before them. Those British wagon wheels were exactly 4-feet 8.5-inches apart because that was the width of ruts in English roads.

British roads were based on roadbeds from the Roman Empire. Ruts in Roman roads were 4-feet 8.5-inches wide because that was the width of the wheels on an ancient chariot. An ancient chariot was that width because that was the breadth of the backsides of two horses harnessed together. So today railroad lines across America are designed on specifications to accommodate the rear ends of Roman horses! Talk about falling into a rut!

How can we climb out of the ruts we sometimes get stuck in? Where can you or I go for a fresh start in a New Year? A real new beginning for a New Year is offered to us this morning in communion. I think the invitation from an old book of worship puts it well. "(You) who do truly and earnestly repent ... of your sins, and are in love and charity with your neighbors, and intend to lead a new life, following the commandments of God and walking from henceforth in (God's) holy ways; draw near with faith, and take this holy Sacrament to your comfort."[1]

"(You) who do truly and earnestly repent ... of your sins." A first step in receiving this Sacrament of new beginnings is confession. As we prepare to receive the Sacrament today we set aside some quiet time for silent confession. Acknowledging our sins is a necessary first step in breaking out of the rut of sin.

In his book *Will Daylight Come?* Richard Hoefler gives an illustration of how sin can enslave us but confession frees us. A boy was visiting his grandparents in the country. While there, someone gave him his first slingshot. Though he practiced in the woods, he could never hit his target. One day as he came into the backyard he spied his grandmother's pet duck.

On an impulse he took a shot at the duck and, to his horror, hit it. The panic-stricken boy picked up the dead duck and tried to hide it in a woodpile. When he looked up he saw his sister Sally watching. She saw everything but said nothing.

That day after lunch his grandmother asked Sally to stay and help her with the dishes. Sally said, "Johnny told me he wanted to help in the kitchen today. Didn't you, Johnny?" Then she whispered in his ear, "Remember the duck." That afternoon a guilty Johnny did the dishes.

Later Sally got Johnny to take her place helping make supper by whispering, "Remember the duck." For several days Sally had Johnny do both his chores and her chores. Finally he couldn't take it any longer. He confessed to his grandmother that he had killed her pet.

"I know, Johnny," she said, giving him a hug. "I was standing at the window and saw the whole thing. Because I love you, I forgave you. I wondered how long you would let Sally make a slave of you."[2]

Sin enslaves. Confession cleanses. A first step toward a new beginning is confessing our sins. "Examine yourselves, and only then eat of the bread and drink of the cup," Paul advises (1 Corinthians 11:28 NRSV). "If we confess our sins, (God) who is

21

faithful and just will forgive us our sins and cleanse us from all unrighteousness," says 1 John (1:9 NRSV).

A second step toward a new beginning is accepting our acceptance. Some of us may have difficulty accepting large gifts. I once spoke with a woman, a member of one of my previous churches, who found herself in that situation. For several years this good-hearted woman had looked after an elderly widow who lived on her street.

She ran errands for the widow and brought her to the doctor. One Memorial Day, she drove the widow to another state to decorate her husband's grave. It was Christian charity with no thought of reward. She was just concerned because she knew the widow was lonely and had no surviving relatives to help.

One day, the widow gave the helpful lady a present and insisted she keep it. It was a diamond broach that had been in her family for many years. It was worth several thousand dollars. The woman took it reluctantly, only because the widow insisted. That broach became something of a problem for her. She was afraid to give it back, lest she hurt the widow's feelings. But she didn't feel right about keeping it, either. She felt she hadn't earned it, she didn't deserve it. The gift seemed too much, too extravagant.

All of us may sometimes feel like that goodhearted woman. We may have trouble accepting lavish gifts we don't feel we've earned. Is it any wonder we sometimes may have trouble accepting, even comprehending God's free gift of salvation?

Yet listen to the testimony of the Apostle Paul, "... God shows his love for us in that while we were yet sinners Christ died for us" (Romans 5:8 RSV). Theologians call that God's prevenient grace. Paul Tillich writes, "You are accepted, accepted by that which is greater than you ... Do not try to do anything now; perhaps later you will seek much. Do not seek anything; do not perform anything; do not intend anything. Simply accept the fact that you are accepted."[3]

The invitation to Communion advises us to "draw near with faith, and take this Holy Sacrament to your comfort." A second step toward a new beginning in a New Year is simply accepting that we are accepted.

A third step is also included in that Communion invitation. Isn't there something about being "in love and charity" with your neighbors and "intending to lead a new life"? There is. After the cleansing of confession and accepting our acceptance comes a call for renewed commitment. As freshly-forgiven people, living in God's grace, and guided and strengthened by the Holy Spirit, we strive to walk again in God's holy ways.

I think there's a universal longing for new beginnings. Perhaps that longing grows stronger around the turn of a New Year. We all can get stuck in a rut. Sometimes sins enslave us. But the good news of the gospel is that Christ has come to set us free. There are steps you and I can take right now toward a New Beginning. Our "do over" day could be today. Let us confess our sins. Let us accept our acceptance. Let us resolve, with God's help, to walk again in God's paths. Let's celebrate this first Communion of a New Year as brothers and sisters in Christ and as God's beloved children. For as hymnist Brian Wren puts it,

In faith we'll gather round the table
to taste and share what love can do.
This is a day of new beginnings
— our God is making all things new.[4]

This is the New Covenant in Christ. This is the day of new beginnings. The real New Year's party is HERE.

1. The General Council of the Congregational Churches, *The Book Of Worship For Free Churches* (New York: Oxford University Press, 1958), p. 107.

2. Craig Brian Larson, *Illustrations For Preaching And Teaching* (Grand Rapids, Michigan: Baker Books, 1993), p. 89 [Richard Hoefler: *Will Daylight Come?*].

3. Paul Tillich, *The Shaking Of The Foundation* (New York: Charles Scribner's Sons, 1948), p. 162.

4. Taken From "This Is A Day Of New Beginnings" © Carol Stream, Illinois: Hope Publishing Company, 1987. All rights reserved. Used by permission.

Called, Commissioned, And Comforted: A Tribute To Dr. Martin Luther King, Jr.

Isaiah 49:1-9

Recently, Rosa Parks was again in the news. You might remember her as the quiet, unassuming, middle-aged black woman with tired feet whose gentle protest on a bus in 1955 helped spark the Civil Rights Movement. This nationally-known figure had been living alone, in poor health, in near poverty, in inner-city Detroit. At age 82, a crack addict broke into her apartment. Rosa Parks was beaten and robbed.

Her situation seemed a sad commentary on the state of black people in America. In the forty years since her protest on a Montgomery, Alabama, bus, things have changed for African-Americans. But they haven't changed enough. One black American in three still lives below the poverty level. Blacks are many times more likely to become the victims of violence than whites. In fact, homicide is the most frequent cause of death for young African-American men. Blacks, representing only eleven percent of the population, now make up over fifty percent of the prisoners in our jails and prisons. Infant mortality rates for black babies are as high as those for some countries in the Third World. Black babies are fourteen times more likely to be born with AIDS. The discrepancies are clear.

Dr. Martin Luther King, Jr., said, "I have a dream, that one day this nation will rise up and live out the true meaning of its creed: we hold these truths to be self-evident; that all men are created equal." Clearly, his vision of equality for all remains a dream. It is not yet a fact.

I know that his reputation has been tarnished some over the years. Still, in spite of his all-too-human failings, Martin Luther King, Jr., remains, to me at least, a great American and an authentic prophet. He fulfills the three characteristics of a prophet written of in Isaiah 49. In this passage, the writer points out that God's prophet is called, commissioned, and comforted. I see evidence of all three of these things in the life of Dr. King.

Verse one of this passage indicates that the authentic prophet is *called*: "Before I was born, the Lord chose me, and appointed me to be his servant." Like the prophet, Martin felt a definite sense of call. "ML," as his family called him, was a brilliant student. He had gone off to Morehouse College in Atlanta at age fifteen. But in his third year, he was still undecided about what profession to pursue. His father, a Baptist minister, wanted Martin to follow him into the ministry. But Martin had been leaning toward either medicine or law. At age seventeen, he experienced a definite call to the ministry. Martin began to pursue this with all his considerable talent and strength. He graduated with honors from Morehouse College at age nineteen. He then went on to attend Crozer Theological Seminary in Chester, Pennsylvania, where he was voted Outstanding Student, receiving straight As all three years. Finally, he completed a Ph.D. at Boston University. He did it all by age 26.

When he graduated, King was offered professorships at two universities and deanship of a small college. He could have had a secure and comfortable teaching career in the North. But instead, in response to his call, he accepted a position as pastor of the 300-member Dexter Avenue Baptist Church in Montgomery, Alabama. Montgomery, you might remember, had been the capital of the Confederacy. It was the deepest Deep South. The Kings' first child, Yolanda, was born while they lived in a run-down parsonage in the ghetto. Martin and Coretta Scott King could have gone almost anywhere. Coretta herself was an accomplished musician with a graduate degree from the New England Conservatory of Music and a promising career. They could have escaped segregation. But they consciously chose to live among their people in response to Martin's call.

26

But according to Isaiah 49, the servant is not only called; he or she is also *commissioned*. In our passage, the Lord speaks to the prophet and commands him to do two things. In verse 9, the prophet is appointed to restore the people of his nation, Israel. But later in the same verse, the prophet's mission is expanded to being a "light" to the nations, a light to *all* people, so that "all the world might be saved." Like the prophet written of in Isaiah, Martin Luther King, Jr.'s, commission unfolded in two parts.

As he began his ministry in Alabama, King was primarily concerned with the plight of black Americans. His earliest challenge was to oppose the discrimination black people experienced on the busses. In the 1950s busses in the South were divided into two sections. Blacks paid their fare in the front of the bus, got off, walked along the curbside, and re-entered through a separate door at the back.

Often the white bus drivers were abusive. Some thought it was funny to drive off after the black passengers had paid their fare but before they could re-board. Sometimes black passengers were threatened with guns. If the busses were crowded, black riders were obligated to give up their seats to whites.

The giving up of their seats is what Rosa Parks protested in 1955. Her feet were tired, and she refused to ride standing up for a young white man. It wasn't even that she wouldn't give up her seat. There were plenty of seats. But the custom was that if even one white person were seated in the black section, all the black passengers were expected to stand. Mrs. Parks simply didn't see why she needed to stand when there were plenty of seats. She was arrested and ordered to pay a fine.

King and other black leaders in Montgomery thought the incident was an outrage. They organized a black boycott of the busses. It was the first large-scale boycott organized in the American South and went on for over a year. In the end, the boycotters won.

Having discovered first-hand the power of nonviolent resistance, King went on to organize freedom marches, boycotts, and lunch counter sit-ins throughout the South. His efforts over ten years were remarkably effective in stirring the conscience of this

27

nation. They prompted the Civil Rights Act of 1964 and the Voting Rights Act of 1965.

King's first concern was for his own people. But like the prophet in Isaiah, King also became a "light" to the nations. His growing international reputation became apparent when he was awarded the Nobel Peace Prize in 1964. He was only 35, the youngest person ever to win that award. In his espousal of non-violent resistance, Martin Luther King, Jr., offered the world an alternative to militarism, terrorism, and war. His principles influenced leaders of the freedom movement in South Africa and the organizers of Solidarity in Poland. The champion of the African-Americans became a light to the world.

The prophet is called. The prophet is commissioned. The prophet is also comforted. In Isaiah, the prophet's discouragement is clear when he writes, "I have worked, but how hopeless it is! I have used up my strength, but have accomplished nothing" (49:4 TEV). Like the prophet, King was no stranger to discouragement. His non-violent resistance cost him a lot.

King was jailed 39 times. Over the years, he and his family received hundreds of death threats, including forty by phone in a single day. Twice his home was bombed, once while his wife and infant daughter were in it. He was clubbed several times on freedom marches. Another time he was stabbed in the chest.

Martin lived almost his entire adult life under the threat of assassination. He began to speak of his own impending death as early as 1955. On the night before he was gunned down in Memphis, King said: "I don't know what will happen now. But it really doesn't matter. Because I've been to the mountaintop. I won't mind. Like anybody, I would like to live a long life. But I'm not concerned about that now. I just want to do God's will. And he's allowed me to go up to the mountain. And I've looked over and seen the Promised Land. I may not get there with you, but I want you to know that we as a people will get to the Promised Land." The next day, April 4, 1968, Martin Luther King, Jr., scholar, preacher, prophet, Nobel Peace Prize winner, father of four young children, was shot to death. He was only 39.

28

Of course King got discouraged. He said in one sermon, "I must admit that at times I have felt I could no longer bear such a heavy burden, and have been tempted to retreat to a more quiet and serene life. But, every time such a temptation appeared, something came to strengthen my determination. I have learned now that the Master's burden is light ... In the midst of dangers, I have felt an inner calm. In the midst of lonely days and dreary nights I have heard an inner voice saying, 'Lo, I will be with you.' When the chains of fear and the manacles of frustration have all but stymied my efforts, I have felt the power of God transforming the fatigue of despair into the buoyancy of hope." He concludes, "I am convinced that the universe is under the control of a loving purpose ... behind the harsh appearance of the world there is a benign power."[1]

Like the authentic prophet, Martin Luther King, Jr., was called, commissioned, and comforted. He never felt that God had abandoned him, even in the midst of mental anguish and physical pain.

I think we do well to set aside a day to remember the example of this American. But just as important as remembering this one man, is remembering that his work is not yet done, and his dream not yet complete.

Only when every Rosa Parks, black or white, is safe and secure in her old age, only when every child, black or white, has hope for the future, only when the hungry are fed and the homeless sheltered and the naked clothed, only when wars and violence cease throughout the earth will we be allowed to celebrate Martin Luther King, Jr., Day completely.

God still needs prophets like Dr. King. God calls us. God gives us specific tasks. God stands by us in our weakness. God laid God's hand on Dr. Martin Luther King, Jr., to serve God. Perhaps God will lay God's hand on you — or me.

---

1. Martin Luther King, Jr., *Strength To Love* (Minneapolis: Fortress, 1986), pp. 152-153.

29

Privilege And Prejudice

1 Corinthians 12:7-13

In 1988, Peggy McIntosh, an administrator at Wellesley College Center for Research on Women, published an essay on white privilege. McIntosh compared the circumstances of her life to those of her African-American colleagues in the same building and line of work. After some deep reflection, and analysis of unearned advantages and disadvantages, she began to see that, as a white academic, she was born with what she calls "an invisible package of unearned assets ..." which she calls "white privilege."

McIntosh describes "white privilege" as "an invisible, weightless knapsack of special provisions, maps, passports, codebooks, visas, clothes, tools and blank checks of unearned assets; which I could count on cashing in on every day, but about which I was 'meant' to remain oblivious."

I have spoken to Peggy McIntosh several times. She asked me to make it clear to you that she compared herself only to African-American women she knew and that her list of unearned advantage is autobiographical. She reminds us that having race or gender or sex or religious privilege does not have anything to do with whether or not you are a nice person. We shouldn't feel defensive about or attacked by this analysis.

Let's make this "invisible knapsack" visible *(come down out of pulpit to floor level, bearing knapsack)*. These are some of the unearned privileges McIntosh found in *her* bag:

She writes:

> *I can, if I wish, arrange to be in the company of people of my race most of the time.*
>
> *If I should need to move, I can be pretty sure of renting or purchasing housing in an area which I can afford and in which I would want to live.*

31

I can be pretty sure that my neighbors in such a location will be neutral or pleasant to me.

I can go shopping alone most of the time, pretty well assured that I will not be followed or harassed.

I can turn on the television or open to the front page of the paper and see people of my race widely represented.

I can be sure that my children will be given curricular materials that testify to the existence of their race.

I can talk with my mouth full and not have people put this down to my color.

I can swear, or dress in secondhand clothes, or not answer letters without having people attribute these choices to the bad morals, the poverty or the illiteracy of my race.

I can do well in a challenging situation without being called a credit to my race.

I am never asked to speak for all the people of my racial group.

I can be pretty sure that if I ask to talk to "the person in charge," I will be facing a person of my race.

If a traffic cop pulls me over or if the IRS audits my tax return, I can be sure I haven't been singled out because of my race.

I can easily buy posters, postcards, picture books, greeting cards, dolls, toys, and children's magazines featuring people of my race.

I am not made acutely aware that my shape, bearing, or body odor will be taken as a reflection on my race.

I can take a job with an affirmative action employer without having co-workers on the job suspect that I got it because of my race.

I can choose blemish cover or bandages in "flesh" color and have them more or less match my skin.[1]

Those are some of the contents Peggy McIntosh found in her invisible knapsack. I wonder if you folks carry around such a knapsack. I believe *I* do.

32

I grew up in a small town where (at least for *me*) race was *never* an issue. There were a few Jewish families and Asian-American families in Hollis, New Hampshire, in the 1950s and '60s. In the spring and fall, Hispanic farm workers were "imported" by the large growers to pick their crops. But, of course, they didn't stay. There were no African-American students in our local high school. None. When I went to college, people of color made up only a tiny percentage of the student body.

Like many white Baby Boomers, I benefited from my parents' accumulated assets. A study found that not only do middle-class blacks today earn only seventy percent of the income of middle-class whites, they also possess only fifteen percent of the accumulated wealth.[2]

Robert Kerry said, "To be white in America is not to have to think about it." My whole life long, I've had the luxury of *not* having had to think about racial issues, unless I wanted to. So I do think I carry around an invisible knapsack of white privilege. It's stuffed with advantages I haven't earned, but can take for granted.

So what? Is that a sin? Does privilege equal prejudice? Not necessarily. After all, I didn't choose to be born white. As Peggy McIntosh said to me, "People who are white benefit from white special privileges whether we're prejudiced or not. It doesn't have to do with whether or not we're nice people. It has to do with having doors opened for us."

But does unearned privilege make me less sensitive to the concerns of people of color? Am I, given my background, more likely to see racial issues as "no big deal," to wonder what all the "fuss" is about, to be less concerned than I should be about racial justice? Probably yes.

Peggy McIntosh's essay calls me to soul-searching and self-examination. It suggests that racism might be subtler, and more pervasive, than it seems. That racism is more than hate crimes; more than defacing synagogues, as our Cape synagogue has been defaced twice in the past two years; more than creating a hate-filled, Ku Klux Klan website, or posting despicable posters on telephone poles in Hyannis. It suggests that racism can be found in "nice people" like me.

33

It suggests to me that just accepting the status quo may be a subtle form of racism. That it might be racism to carry around my invisible knapsack, and never dump it out and see what's inside. That it might be racism not to care "Is this fair?," not to speak up, not to speak out about my unearned advantage.

Martin Luther King, Jr., wrote, "The greatest tragedy ... (is) not the strident clamor of the bad people, but the appalling silence of the good people."[3]

He wrote, "It is appalling that the most segregated hour of Christian America is eleven o'clock on Sunday morning, the same hour when many are standing to sing 'In Christ There is No East or West.' "[4] He wrote, "Injustice anywhere is a threat to justice everywhere."[5]

Thirty-five years ago he wrote, in "Letter from Birmingham City Jail":

> *I have been so greatly disappointed with the white Church and its leadership ... here we are moving toward the exit of the twentieth century with a religious community largely adjusted to the status quo, standing as a tail light behind other community agencies rather than a headlight leading men to higher levels of justice ... If the Church of today does not recapture the sacrificial spirit of the early Church, it will lose its authentic ring ... and be dismissed as an irrelevant social club....*[6]

The prophet's voice, King's voice, still rings, and stings today. Have we in the white church become too comfortable, too complacent with our invisible knapsacks? Are we a headlight or a taillight working for racial justice? Are our hearts open, or have we grown deaf to the cries of our sisters and brothers?

Another prophet, W. E. B. DuBois, from Western Massachusetts, stated in 1900 that "the problem of the twentieth century is the problem of the color line." Will racism be "the problem" of the twenty-first century as well? Will you and I and this church be part of the problem, or part of the solution?

34

These are some of the questions I ask myself on Martin Luther King, Jr., Sunday, near the beginning of a new year, at the edge of a new millennium. There are questions for us in our worship bulletins:

- What do you think about the "invisible knapsack of white privilege"?
- If you have a knapsack, what's in yours? Can you illustrate?
- What can we, as individuals and as a church, do to combat racism and prejudice?
- Are there any other thoughts or experiences you would care to share?

---

1. Used by permission. All quotes from "White Privilege and Male Privilege: a Personal Account of Coming to See Correspondence through Work in Women's Studies," published by Wellesley College Centers for Women, or its excerpt, "White Privilege: Unpacking the Invisible Knapsack," *Peace and Freedom* magazine, July/August, 1989. For permission to excerpt or quote, reprint must be obtained from Peggy McIntosh, Wellesley Centers for Women, Wellesley, Massachusetts 02481. Telephone 781-283-2522, FAX 781-283-2504.

2. Melvin L. Oliver and Thomas N. Shapiro, *Black Wealth, White Wealth* (London: Routledge Press, 1997), p. 7.

3. Martin Luther King, Jr., *Stride Toward Freedom* (New York: Harper and Brothers, 1958), p. 202.

4. *Ibid.*, p. 207.

5. *Ibid.*, p. 199.

6. Martin Luther King, Jr., "Letter From Birmingham City Jail" printed in American Friends Service Committee booklet, 1963, pp. 11-12.

Going For The Goal
In Football And Faith

Hebrews 12:1-3, 12a

I caught the title out of the corner of my eye while wandering through a bookstore. The title was so surprising I stopped in my tracks to look at the book. Here it is. It's titled *Fitness Is Religion: Keep the Faith* (Simon and Schuster). *Fitness* is *religion.* Keep the *faith!* With an introduction by (of *all* people) Madonna! The connection between fitness and faith, religion, and a raucous rock star was startling to me. So I ordered the book on interlibrary loan.

Fitness Is Religion: Keep the Faith did not disappoint me. The author, Ray Kybartas, is personal trainer to the stars. He uses a number of religious metaphors to explain his philosophy of fitness. To Ray Kybartas, working out is "going to church." "Exercise is prayer." "Diet" is "a sacrament." People who exercise regularly (religiously) are "converts." Couch potatoes are "unbelievers." Committing to an exercise program is taking "a leap of faith."[1]

Sometimes we see sports and religion as rivals, don't we? Clergy types (like me) can complain about Michael Jordan being marketed like a minor god. Or about the outrageous salaries paid to professional athletes — tens of millions of dollars — money that could go to charity. Or about fans who spend more time watching sports than they do attending worship.

All true: a person *can* become excessively addicted to sports. Reminds me of a story I once heard:

> *A man was seated next to the only empty seat in the stadium on Super Bowl Sunday. The hot dog vendor couldn't help but notice the empty seat.*
>
> *"Hey, how come that seat's empty?" asked the vendor.*

The guy replied, "That's my wife's seat."

"Where's she?" asked the vendor.

"She's dead."

"I'm sorry," said the hot dog guy. "But that's a $400 seat. This is the biggest game of the year! Couldn't you find a friend or a relative to use her ticket?"

"Nah!" said the husband. "They're all at her funeral."[2]

We *can* put sports ahead of everything, including marriage, family, *and* God. That's idolatry. Still, sports and religion don't have to be rivals, do they? On this Super Bowl Sunday, I'd like to explore the possible connections between sports and religion, especially the possible connections between football and faith.

For one thing, there are almost semi-religious rituals in football, aren't there? An unknown author once pointed some of them out. This author writes:

Obviously, football is a syndrome of religious rites symbolizing the struggle to preserve the egg of life through the rigors of ... winter ... In these rites, the egg of life is symbolized by an oval-shaped inflated bladder covered with pig skin. The egg motif is repeated in the ... oval design of the vast outdoor churches in which services are held every (Sunday) ... Literally millions of worshipers attend the Sabbath services in these enormous outdoor churches ... the rites are performed on a rectangular area of green ... The grass, symbolizing summer, is striped with ominous white lines representing the knifing snows of winter....

The ceremony begins with colorful processions of musicians and semi-nude maidens ... This excites the thousands of worshipers to rise from their seats ... the rites are performed by 22 young priests of perfect physique ... The group in ... possession of the oval first arrange themselves in an egg-shaped huddle ... for a moment of prayerful meditation and whispering of secret numbers....[3]

38

The ball as the "egg of life"; the field as summer knifed by the snows of winter; the four quarters of the game representing the seasons; semi-nude maidens; players as priests — and much of it done in the name of "Alma Mater," "Dear Mother." Football *does* sound a bit like an ancient, pagan religious rite!

But others have applied football imagery to worship. "Blocking" becomes talking too long with the pastor at the door after church, holding up the line. "Extra point" is what you get when you tell the preacher her sermon was *too short*. "Interference" is talking during the prelude. "Illegal motion" is leaving before the service is over. "Passing game" is what latecomers do when the person at the end of the pew won't slide over. "Quarterback" is what a cheapskate wants after putting a half dollar into the offering. "Two minute warning" is people looking at their watches during the sermon.[4]

There *are* humorous connections between faith and football — but also serious ones. For one thing, faith and football both require commitment. You can bet the players on winning teams are seriously committed to the goal of getting a Super Bowl Ring.

Both teams have trained hard all season. But you can bet they have trained harder these past few days (at least since Thursday — many of them partied earlier in the week). Remembering plays, running plays, wind sprints, pushups, sit-ups, stomach crunches, playing through injuries. Football requires commitment. Players understand the saying, "No pain, no gain."

But doesn't *faith* also require commitment? The Apostle Paul employed athletic images to describe our spiritual journeys. Paul writes: "Every athlete in training submits to strict discipline, in order to be crowned (with the victory wreath) ... That is why I run straight for the finish line; that is why I am like a boxer who does not waste his punches. I harden my body with blows and bring it under complete control ..." (1 Corinthians 9:24-27a TEV). "No pain, no gain" was a byword for the Apostle Paul.

Someone once said, "Faith is like a muscle. It grows stronger the more we use it." The late Mother Teresa weighed less than 100 pounds. She stood less than five feet tall. But while she couldn't have played defensive tackle, she was a worldwide power for good

39

because of her faith. Both football and faith require commitment. I wonder: What might *we* accomplish as individuals, what might *we* accomplish as a congregation *if* we invested an athlete's effort in the daily exercise of our faith?

But while football and faith both demand commitment, they also both rely on grace. Not the grace of a quarterback weaving his way through a field of tacklers, but "grace" as a power that comes from beyond ourselves. Many great players will tell you that they can't do what they do on their own. There are moments when they feel "captured" by a higher power.

Chicago Bears great "Red" Grange was called "The Galloping Ghost" for his fleetness of foot. A reporter once asked "Red" Grange how he managed to elude tacklers. This was "The Galloping Ghost's" response:

> *I can't explain it or take credit for it. You can teach a man how to block or tackle, run or pass, but you can't teach a man how to run so tacklers won't tackle him. No one ever taught me, and I can't teach anyone. If you can't explain it, how can you take credit for it?*[5]

"Red" Grange was saying he couldn't take credit for his game. He received his special ability as a gift. It came from beyond himself.

Like "Red" Grange people of faith are also graced by a higher power. Christians call it the Holy Spirit. We receive it at baptism. There are moments when, through the grace of God and the power of the Holy Spirit, we manage to say just the right thing, or do just the right thing, or not do the wrong thing. We make a bad situation better, or relieve suffering, or witness for Jesus.

But in that instant, you know it's not you who is doing it. You are being used. It's not so much you are living your faith as the Holy Spirit is living through you. What a blessing it is when God chooses to use us as a channel for God's Holy Spirit! Football and faith demand commitment, but both depend on grace.

Also, in football, as in faith, we need each other. No football player can go it alone. Each player needs the other members on the team to be successful, and each team includes players with a

40

variety of differing gifts. Quarterbacks, halfbacks, and fullbacks, defensive players, offensive players, specialty teams, kickers all are necessary. So, the quarterback has no right to look down on the line. In fact, he *needs* their blocking if he is to survive. So it is in Christ's church. There are many parts — many members — but one body. Each member is necessary for the health of the body (see 1 Corinthians 12:12ff). That's why we're so blessed to receive thirteen new members. That's why *each* of you is necessary for the healthy functioning of this church.

Sometimes our job is to cheer each other on, like the crowd in the stadium cheers on the exhausted runner in this morning's scripture. Sometimes our job is to call each other back. Not the longest but the "wrongest" run in football took place in the 1929 Rose Bowl game. California was leading Georgia Tech seven to six. California player Roy Riegels got the ball. He became confused and began running in the wrong direction. The crowd shouted, "Wrong way, Roy! Wrong way, Roy!" He thought they were cheering him on and ran faster. Finally one of his own teammates tackled him on the one-yard line. But, it was too late, California fumbled the punt. Georgia Tech won.

In the church, sometimes we need each other to cheer us on. Sometimes we need each other to call us back when we're heading in the wrong direction. But what's important *is* that we need each other. Football and faith are team efforts, and in both football *and* faith, we are headed for a goal.

Paul writes, "... forgetting what lies behind and straining forward to what lies ahead, I press on toward the goal for the prize of the upward call of God in Christ Jesus" (Philippians 3:13b-14 RSV). I hope we all understand that faith, like football, demands commitment. But faith, like football, depends on grace. Plus in faith *and* in football, we need each other — and that both faith and football are going for a goal.

In 1920, at age 25, George Gipp, Notre Dame's star player, died of pneumonia. On his deathbed, George Gipp spoke to Knute Rockne, his coach. He said, "Someday, when things look real tough for Notre Dame, ask the boys to go out there and win one for the Gipper."

41

Jesus also died young, but on the third day God raised him up from the dead with mighty power. Jesus is alive even now. He has already won the Big One for us, the big victory over sin and death. He just calls us to keep on winning the small victories *against* sin and *for* love every day.

As someone said, God calls us together into a "holy huddle." God calls us to keep on winning, not for the "Gipper," but for Christ. On this Super Bowl Sunday, let us recommit ourselves to going for the goal of loving, honoring, and serving Jesus, helping each other and relying on the power of God's Holy Spirit, until the goal is fulfilled and God's will is done on earth as it is in heaven. Enjoy the game!

---

1. Ray Kybartas, *Fitness Is Religion: Keep the Faith* (New York: Simon and Schuster, 1997), pp. 14, 34, 33, 34, 21.

2. Unknown.

3. Edward K. Powell, editor, *Humor For Preaching And Teaching* (Grand Rapids, Michigan: Baker Books, 1996), pp. 158-159.

4. *Ibid.*, Powell.

5. Clifton Fadiman, editor, *The Little Brown Book Of Anecdotes* (Boston: Little, Brown, and Company, 1985), p. 252.

Valentines

1 Corinthians 12:31b—13:8a, 13

Back in February of 1848, Esther Howland, a student at Mount Holyoke Seminary for Females (now Mount Holyoke College), sat in her dorm room and cut dozens of little hearts out of paper. After she had cut them out, she trimmed the edges with bits of lace. Then she wrote a high-minded sentiment at the center of each heart and gave them as gifts to friends and family. Her little creations became wildly popular. Soon Esther, a resourceful sort, had organized a crew of other students into an assembly line to cut out and trim her valentines. With that, according to historian Frances Cagnon, the American valentine industry was born.

Today, Valentine's Day brings retailers billions of dollars. We exchange a billion valentines a year in this country alone. They come in thousands of different styles — Hallmark, in one recent year, made 2,100 different kinds of valentines. They come with a variety of sayings. Some valentines are sweet: "To a very special Daddy from your very special little lamb." Others are sentimental: "For Baby's first valentine." Some are sarcastic. You might call them "vinegar valentines." They have lines like "Ours is a strange and wonderful relationship; I'm wonderful and you're strange!" Or like the card *I* once received: "I've been thinking a lot about you on Valentine's Day, which is strange ... because I don't usually think about you until April Fool's Day!" Some valentines are musical. Others are funny. I once read one that said on the outside, "When I was little, I used to tell my innermost secrets to my Teddy Bear; But now I've got *you* to confide in." The inside read: "Poor Teddy. He knew too much, so I had to get rid of him. Happy Valentine's Day!" Some valentines are sexy. I remember once taking our son, when he was *much* younger, over to a local drugstore to pick out a valentine for my wife, Bonnie. While

43

I wasn't looking, he wandered over to the adult rack and came back with a few valentines he didn't understand. "I don't get it Dad. What does this one mean...?" Followed by a moment of parental silence.

Valentines can be sweet, sentimental, sarcastic, or sexy. Who would have guessed that they were originally designed to celebrate not romantic love, but the life of a Christian saint? You may know that valentines get their name from Saint Valentine, a Christian bishop and martyr who lived in the third century during a time when Rome was persecuting the church. Bishop Valentine disobeyed one of the laws. The Emperor, Claudius the Second, had decreed that, throughout the Empire, the marriage of healthy military-age men should be discouraged. It was his opinion that married men wouldn't make good soldiers because they would be too worried about their families to fight.

Valentine disagreed with the law and continued to perform marriages for young Christian couples. For his civil disobedience, he was thrown into jail. While in prison, Valentine, who could read and write in a day when most people couldn't, used to write letters on behalf of the other prisoners to their loved ones on the outside. Since he had acted as scribe, he would sign the letters, "From your Valentine." For his continuing help to people in need, at considerable risk to himself, and for his original disobedience, Valentine was tortured and killed on February 14.

Beginning in the Middle Ages, believers used to exchange cards on February 14 in remembrance of this saint and martyr. These original valentines were tribute not to sentimentality, but to courage and self-sacrifice in the Christian life. We apparently have lost a lot of the original meaning of Valentine's Day, just as we have lost a lot of the original meaning of Christmas. Valentine's Day was first designed to celebrate Christian love, not romantic love.

Both are important, of course, and *both* worthy of celebration. But there *is* a considerable difference between the two. For one thing, scientists are discovering that romantic love, particularly in its early stages, is largely a matter of chemicals. When we're interested in someone, infatuated, "struck by Cupid's arrow," when we feel a little bit silly and maybe a little bit giddy in that special person's presence, our brain is releasing some natural amphetamines. These stimulants produce powerful feelings of elation and euphoria. Unfortunately, after two or three years, the affect of these chemicals begins to wane. That's why, *worldwide*, the largest number of couples divorce in the fourth year of marriage, *after* the brain chemicals have begun to wear off. Fortunately, these original chemicals are eventfully replaced by other chemicals, endorphins, which are similar in their makeup to morphine. These endorphins can provide lovers in longtime relationships with the feelings of calm, security, and peace that they often find in each other's company.

Romantic love may not be so much a result of cupid's arrows as it is a matter of chemistry! In fact we do talk about the "chemistry" between two people. But Christian love, agape love, is *more than* chemistry. Christian love is an act of the will: being patient and kind, not jealous or boastful, or arrogant or rude, not insisting on having our own way, not being irritable or resentful, bearing all things, believing all things, hoping all things, enduring all things. At its best, Christian love, unlike some chemically induced euphoria, "never ends." Plus, it's extended, not just to people we like or find attractive, but to everyone, even to people we don't know, even to those who have hurt us, disappointed us, or betrayed us.

Why? Not necessarily because we have warm, fuzzy feelings for these folks, but because of our gratitude for what *God* has done for us. We love because we have first been loved, by God in Christ. God is "patient and kind" to us, although we turn away from God daily. God's love for us "bears all things, believes all things, hopes all things, endures all things." God's love for us "never ends." It may be easier to love others if we reflect on how graciously we have been treated by God.

Victor Hugo, in his classic, *Les Miserables*, demonstrates how an act of Christian love can change things. The main character of the novel, as you may remember from the book or the musical, is Jean Valjean. He is poor and hungry and steals a loaf of bread. For that minor crime, he is imprisoned in a harsh prison for seven years. He comes out a hardened and angry man who, as an ex-con, has trouble fitting in. Jean Valjean is not particularly attractive or likable.

45

One night he goes to the home of Bienvenu, a bishop. He's given a meal and invited to stay the night. While everyone is asleep, Jean Valjean prowls the house, finds some silver candlesticks and silverware and steals the silverware. He runs out into the street but is caught by the gendarmes. They recognize the silverware as belonging to the bishop and bring Jean back.

But the bishop has seen something in Jean Valjean that no one has seen. He tells the police a surprising thing. He says Jean didn't steal the silver. It was a gift. And he asks Jean why he didn't take the silver candlesticks as well.

Let me read you Victor Hugo's wonderful portrayal of this scene:

> *Jean Valjean was trembling in every limb. He took the two candlesticks mechanically and with a wild appearance.*
>
> *"Now," said the bishop, "go in peace. By the way, my friend, when you come again, you need not come through the garden. You can always come in and go out by the front door. It is closed only with a latch, day or night."*
>
> *Then turning to the gendarmes, he said: "Messieurs, you can retire." The gendarmes withdrew.*
>
> *Jean Valjean felt like a man who is just about to faint.*
>
> *The bishop approached him, and said, in a low voice: "Forget not, never forget that you have promised me to use this silver to become an honest man."*
>
> *Jean Valjean, who had no recollection of this promise, stood confounded. The bishop had laid much stress upon these words as he uttered them. He continued, solemnly: "Jean Valjean, my brother: you belong no longer to evil, but to good. It is your soul that I am buying for you ... and I give it to God!"*[1]

I find that a moving scene. In the novel, the bishop is a Christ figure. He loved Jean Valjean with Christian love. He saw good in him. He forgave his sin. He trusted him. He made it possible for Jean Valjean to begin again — which he did.

Remember, Jesus has done *all* those things for me — and you. He has loved us, trusted us, seen good in us, "bought our souls" on the cross and given them back. Now he simply asks us to love one another with *his* kind of love.

In the midst of all the hearts and roses and lace and candy and wonderful sentimentality of Valentine's Day, could we spare a moment to remember Saint Valentine, a Christian bishop and martyr? For our world needs "valentines" who will "resist the power of evil," social evil, and "visit the prisoner," and comfort the dispirited, as Valentine did. It needs "valentines," like Bishop Bienvenu, who will see good in the unlovely and love the unlovely until they can begin to love themselves. Can we strive not just to *give* valentines, but to *be* valentines?

That could be our Valentine's Day gift back to God, who "cared enough to send the very best."

---

1. Victor Hugo, *Les Miserables* (New York: Coronet Press, 1862), p. 90.

47

First In War, First In Peace

Psalm 1

Peter Gibbon is an author, lecturer, and much-quoted researcher at Harvard University. Dr. Gibbon has written articles on, and speaks on "The End of Admiration." He laments the loss of what he calls "public heroes" in America. Today we know so much about prominent individuals, and especially about their shortcomings, that sometimes it's hard to look up to anyone anymore.

Thomas Jefferson is identified as "the president with the slave mistress." Mozart is remembered at "the careless genius who talked dirty." We see film clips of George Bush (the elder) getting sick in public, Dan Quayle misspelling "potato," Gerald Ford stumbling, or Bill Clinton denying. "In a wired world with no restraint, we know the worst about everyone instantly," Gibbon contends.[1]

Maybe it *is* harder today to hold up heroes. Perhaps that's one reason George Washington doesn't seem to receive much attention anymore. Almost fifty years ago, when I was a child, our first president was held in general admiration. Around this time of year we carefully studied his example in school. We sang songs about "George Washington, the father of our country." But starting in 1971, his birthday was folded in with Lincoln's to create "Presidents' Day." Most years this holiday seems little more than a day off from work or school and an opportunity for sales at the mall. On this Sunday closest to Washington's birthday, I'd like to reflect on the legacy he left us. There are significant reasons to admire this man.

One thing I admire about Washington is his lifelong concern over his reputation and character. Actually, the story we learned as children, about the boy George cutting down a cherry tree with his little hatchet, then refusing to tell a lie to his father — that famous story about telling the truth isn't true. It was made up long after

Washington's death by an Anglican clergyman named Parson Weems. Weems wasn't really seeking to deceive anyone. He just needed a lesson for schoolchildren.

But it is true that Washington was a man of great civility and integrity. Like many in his age, he made a careful study of morality and manners. One of his chief guides in life was "The Rules of Civility and Decent Behavior in Company and in Conversation." These rules were based on the work of French Jesuits compiled in 1595. Washington copied each of the 110 rules of civility by hand when he was sixteen. He spent the remaining 61 years of his life trying to live them out.

Some of the rules were crude. Rule number nine was "Spit not into the fire ... nor set your feet upon the fire, especially if there is meat before it." But the principle behind every rule was disclosed in the first: "Every action done in company ought to be done with some sign of respect to those that are present." That's a good paraphrase of the Golden Rule: "... do unto others as you would have them do unto you" (Matthew 7:12 NRSV). Washington's principle guideline was respect for others. His civility and good manners were legendary, especially during his presidency, even though Washington struggled all his life to keep his considerable temper under control.

One of Washington's other virtues was courage. Most of us know something about his bravery under fire. For example, in 1755, when he was just 23, Washington was in a battle in the French and Indian War (this time fighting *with* the British). Two horses were shot out from under him. His hat was shot off. Bullets tore his coat. He continued to fight.

But just as impressive was his courage in the face of personal adversity. Washington didn't have an easy life. His infant sister died when he was eight. His half-brother also died prematurely. The family home in Virginia burned down one Christmas Eve. When Washington was eleven, his father died, and the family's survival was threatened. From age eleven onward he grew up in a single-parent home, very difficult in those days.

His health was also precarious. Though a strapping six-foot-three-and-a-half inches tall (in a time when the average man was

50

five-feet-seven) and an excellent athlete, he suffered from small-pox, tuberculosis, and bouts of dysentery and malaria. Especially when ill, he showed signs of depression. But through it all he pushed on. He had courage in the face of adversity.

Biographer Richard Brookhiser writes that Washington was concerned not only for his own character but also with that of our developing country. At one point after the Revolution the president wrote, "We have now a national character to establish, and it is of the utmost importance to stamp favorable impressions upon it."[2]

He also upheld high standards in foreign relations. Washington wrote in his "Farewell Address": "Observe good faith and justice toward all nations. Cultivate peace and harmony with all...." The hero who fought and won the Revolutionary War, who said "To be prepared for war is one of the most effectual means of preserving peace," also lead our nation in eight years of peace. Washington was not only "first in war" but also "first in peace."

As Psalm 1 puts it, "Happy are those who do not follow the advice of the wicked, or take the path that sinners tread, or sit in the seat of scoffers; but their delight is in the law of the Lord, and on his law they meditate day and night" (vv. 1-2 NRSV). There is truth that happiness comes through self-mastery. We could do worse than hold up George Washington as an example for admiration, as someone who, in good and bad circumstances, strove to develop and perfect himself.

Another thing noteworthy to me about Washington is his balanced views on religion. Washington, by nature, was a shy and reserved person. He was reticent about sharing his views on religion. However, Washington was quite open about his belief that God oversees and guides our national life. After being sworn in as president, his first official act was to join with members of the House and Senate in a two-hour worship service. The president worshiped at an Episcopal church every Sunday (although, like many of the founding fathers, he had deistic leanings and rarely took communion). Throughout his eight years in office, Washington stressed God's providence and guidance. In his "Farewell Address" he wrote,

51

"Of all the dispositions and habits which lead to political prosperity, religion and morality are indispensable supports."[3]

Washington knew the importance of religion. He was also well aware of the danger of religious fanatics. He wrote in a letter to a friend, "Religious controversies are always productive of more acrimony and hatreds than those that spring from any other cause."

Like the other founding fathers, Washington promoted freedom of religion. He himself was religiously tolerant. During the Revolutionary War, he ordered an end to the celebration of "Pope's Day" in the Continental Army. On Pope's Day, Protestants would mock Roman Catholics by burning an effigy of the Pope. Washington made it stop.

On another occasion, when asked by an overseer at Mount Vernon what kind of workers to hire, Washington wrote, "If they are good workmen, they may be from Asia, Africa, or Europe; they may be Mahometans, Jews, Christians of any sect, or they may be Atheists...." He had his own religious beliefs, but was tolerant of others. We have benefited from his balanced position on religion.

A final thing I admire about Washington is his humility. He was so popular at the end of the Revolutionary War that many of his countrymen wanted to make him king. Yet Washington, the only American president to be unanimously elected, in his eight years of office, ignored most of the trappings of power (although he did love to ride; he knew he was a striking figure on a horse and often rode a white horse with a gold-trimmed saddle). One of his legacies was not seeking a third term — a pattern followed by every president up to F. D. Roosevelt, and now enshrined in the 22nd Amendment.

Washington's humility was equally evident earlier. Once, during the Revolutionary War, he was out riding in civilian clothes. Washington came upon a non-commissioned officer bullying a squad of soldiers digging a ditch. The man shouted commands and cursed, but wasn't helping. Washington asked him why.

The man pulled himself up to his full height and said, with dignity, "Sir, I am a corporal." Washington got off his horse and pitched in digging the ditch. When the job was done he got back

52

on his horse and said to the corporal, "Mr. Corporal, next time you have a job like this and not enough men to do it, go to your Commander-in-Chief and I will help you again." Too late the corporal recognized the officer as Washington.[4]

At another point he faced down a potential mutiny with just his glasses. The year was 1783. The Revolutionary War was over. But many American officers were still owed back pay, some up to six years. A group headquartered in Newburgh, New York, was planning a revolt.

Washington was warned of the plot and paid an unexpected visit to the officers. He made a brief speech, which was greeted with irritation and suspicion. Then he produced a letter, which he said was from Congress. He fumbled with the letter, and readjusted it before his eyes several times. The assembled officers were puzzled by Washington's delay. Finally he reached into and pulled out a new pair of glasses. He had never worn his glasses in public before.

He said, "Gentlemen, you will permit me to put on my spectacles, for I have not only grown gray but almost blind in the service of my country." Eyes misted and hearts lifted as the rebellious officers realized again what their Commander-in-Chief had sacrificed for them and their country. The potential mutiny fell apart.

George Washington's example still is admirable, especially today when in America there is a renewed interest in virtue ethics. I find him a good illustration of the importance of seeking right living and a good character. He was likewise wise in his promotion of religion, balanced by an awareness of its dangers and excesses. His personal humility is impressive for a man of his stature.

George Washington was, as Representative Richard Henry Lee said in Washington's eulogy, "First in war, first in peace, and first in the hearts of his countrymen." Earlier generations called him "The American Moses," "American icon," and "our patron Saint." We're well beyond that kind of near idolatrous hero worship today. Still, I think there's something about this man's faith and character that deserves our admiration, especially in a time that seems to be lacking public heroes.

53

1. Dr. Peter Gibbon, "The End Of Admiration," printed in *Imprimis* Journal (Hillsdale, Michigan: Hillsdale College, 1999), pp. 1-4.

2. Richard Brookhiser, *Founding Father* (New York: The Free Press, 1997), p. 133.

3. For specifics on Washington's faith, see *George Washington and Religion*, by Paul E. Boller, Jr., (Dallas, Texas: Southern Methodist University Press, 1963).

4. Clifton Fadiman, editor, *The Little Brown Book Of Anecdotes* (Boston: Little, Brown, and Company, 1985), p. 571.

The Faith Of Abraham

Hebrews 11:1, 8-16

Let me begin this sermon on this Sunday before Presidents' Day by telling what Abraham Lincoln called "his favorite story." There were *lots* of stories about Lincoln in the newspapers when he was president. But *this* is the one Abe said he enjoyed most:

> *Two Quaker women were talking about who would win the Civil War — President Lincoln for the United States or Jefferson Davis for the Confederacy. The first Quaker woman declared she thought Jeff Davis would win.*
>
> *"Why thinkest thou that?" asked the second.*
>
> *The first Quaker woman replied, "Because Jefferson Davis is a praying man."*
>
> *"But, Abraham Lincoln is a praying man, also!" replied the second.*
>
> *"Yes," retorted the first, "but the Lord will think Abraham is joking."*

We know a *lot* about Lincoln, don't we? We know about his birth in a log cabin in the backwoods of Kentucky. We know about his lack of formal education, about his feats of strength, splitting rails or wrestling bullies. We know about his honesty, walking miles to return six overcharged pennies.

We know a *lot* about Lincoln. But, how much do we know about his faith? Do we know he was, as the story puts it, "a praying man"? Do we know how much his faith directed his actions? Willard Sperry, Dean of Harvard Divinity School, often referred to Lincoln as a "theologian." Reinhold Niebuhr, himself one of America's greatest theologians, called Lincoln the most original of all American religious thinkers. What was there about the faith of Abraham Lincoln that helped make him a great *religious* figure in these men's eyes?

For one thing, Abraham Lincoln was "steeped in the Bible." Elton Trueblood, a noted preacher and author writes, "Biblical language was so deeply embedded in (Lincoln's) mind that it became his normal way of speaking."[1]

The importance of the Bible to Lincoln is noted in Richard Swanson's compilation of anecdotes and sketches of Lincoln.

> *The first twenty-one years of my life totaled one year of formal schooling. I got the bulk of my education by self study and by necessity. I read some books; didn't read many 'cause they were just too scarce. Books I did read, though, well, I read them over and over again. You might say I really 'squeezed the juice' out of them. First book I remember reading was Weems'* Life of George Washington. *Later I read* Aesop's Fables, Pilgrim's Progress, Robinson Crusoe, Arabian Nights, Dillworth Spelling Book, *and the* Bible. *The* Bible *had a big impact on my life. Might say I read it backward and forward. I memorized large quantities of it and used much of it in my speeches and writing. Always felt that the* Bible *was God's greatest gift to man and one should take all he could from the book, based on reason and balanced on faith and he'd live and die a better person.*[2]

Obviously, the faith of Abraham had a strong foundation in knowledge of and respect for *the Bible*. Biblical phrases, allusions and quotations appear over and over in Lincoln's speeches, as in the Gettysburg Address, where he begins "Fourscore and seven years ago," echoing Psalm 90.

Another important element of Lincoln's faith was his prayer life. Trueblood writes of him, "He prayed alone, and he called the nation to prayer; he prayed for guidance, and he prayed in gratitude; he prayed in defeat, and he prayed in victory. Often noted was his reverence when others engaged in vocal prayer."[3] Lincoln said himself, "I have been driven many times to my knees by the overwhelming conviction that I had nowhere else to go." The faith of Abraham included a belief in the power of prayer.

Even though he studied the scriptures, apparently daily, and was a man of prayer, Abraham Lincoln never became a church member. As president, he did worship at the New York Avenue Presbyterian Church in Washington, D.C., but never joined. According to Swanson, here are Lincoln's own words:

> *I believe in God and I studied the scriptures. But, I never united myself with any particular church. And that really bothered folks in my day. But, I just found it difficult giving my assent to the long and complicated statements of Christian doctrine that were characterized by their articles of belief and confessions of faith. I could have readily embraced a church whose sole qualification for membership was "Thou shalt love the Lord thy God with all thy heart, all thy soul, all thy mind and thy neighbor as thyself." But, in lieu of that, I went along with that old man who stood up in church one day and he said, "When I do good, I feel good; and when I do bad, I feel bad, and that's my religion."*
>
> *This religious issue was a cloud that hung over my head all my life. In 1860, when I was making a run for President, seventeen of the nineteen Protestant ministers in Springfield, Illinois, voted against me. They felt I was an atheist, agnostic, infidel, nonbeliever. Well, so be it.*[4]

Church member or not, Lincoln was a man of faith. His faith pulled him through many losses and disappointments: including the death of his mother when Lincoln was only seven, the death of two of his sons before his own death and many, many other painful moments. Francis Carpenter, who painted him, said Lincoln had "the saddest face I have ever painted." Yet, in this letter to a little girl who had lost her father, Lincoln explains how faith could see her through:

57

Dear Fanny:

It is with deep grief that I learn of the death of your kind and brave father; and, especially, that it is affecting your young heart beyond what is common in such cases. In this sad world of ours, sorrow comes to all; and, to the young, it comes with bitterest agony, because it takes them unawares. The older have learned to ever expect it. I am anxious to afford some alleviation of your present distress. Perfect relief is not possible, except with time. You can not now realize that you will ever feel better. Is not this so? And yet it is a mistake. You are sure to be happy again. To know this, which is certainly true, will make you some less miserable now. I have had experience enough to know what I say; and you need only to believe it to feel better at once. The memory of your dear father, instead of an agony, will yet be a sad, sweet feeling in your heart, of a purer and holier sort that you have known before.[5]

That's the most important implication, I think, to the faith of Abraham. This man's faith made a difference, not only for himself but even more importantly, for a generation, for a nation, for the entire world. Lincoln more than just introduced the phrase, in the Gettysburg Address, that we are a nation "under God." It's more than just "In God We Trust" first being stamped on our coins in his administration. Lincoln *really* did trust God, tried to know God, tried to know God's will for himself and for our country and tried to *do* God's will. Lincoln once said, "In the very responsible position in which I happen to be placed, being a humble instrument in the hands of our Heavenly Father ... to work out his great purposes, I have desired that all my works and acts may be according to his will...."

Lincoln was *hungry* to do God's will. He wanted our *nation* to do God's will. He once said, quoting Jefferson, "I tremble for my country when I remember God is just." He wanted our whole *nation's* efforts to be invested in trying to know and do God's will. So he called this nation nine times to days of public thanksgiving or public penance, fasting, and prayer. Lincoln realized personal

58

faith was not enough. Faith had to be lived out in the stresses and strains of public life.

That's something of what is meant by "The Faith of Abraham." It's trying to discover God's will for us, as best we can, through prayer and scripture; reason and conscience. It's not just believing in God in some general way but actually trying do God's will, wherever that may lead. It's trusting God, even when things get pretty grim for us.

The faith of Abraham: you don't have to be a Lincoln to have it. And Lincoln didn't have it all at once. It developed over years as he struggled with his conscience.

The faith of Abraham; it's called for still. For there continue to be many threats to the health and survival of our nation. And injustice — racial injustice, economic injustice, continues still.

Let us then, in the words of Lincoln, "strive on to finish the work we are in." Let us, again in Lincoln's words, be determined "to do all which may achieve and cherish a just, and lasting peace, among ourselves and with all nations."

---

1. Elton Trueblood, *Abraham Lincoln: Theologian Of American Anguish* (New York: Harper and Row, 1973), p. 49.

2. Richard Swanson, *That Reminds Me Of A Story: The Life Of Abraham Lincoln* (privately published, 1995), used by permission from a taped presentation given at my church.

3. Trueblood, *ibid.*, p. 73.

4. Swanson, *ibid.*

5. Swanson, *ibid.*

Christ In All Things: The Faith Of Saint Patrick

Romans 5:1-5

On this Saint Patrick's Day I'd like to begin the sermon with an Irish greeting: "Cead Mile Failta" (pronounced keed mila felt-ya). That's my best Irish for "A hundred thousand welcomes," which, they tell me at the Keltic Kitchen, is the appropriate way to greet any large assembly (whether there happen to be 100,000 people or not). As you might have guessed, I'm *not* Irish myself. Still, on Saint Patrick's Day, many of us like to be at least a little bit "Irish." I once read a newspaper article listing ten things anyone could do to be authentically Irish on Saint Patrick's Day. The article went something like this:

1. *Drink a pot of tea.*
2. *... Start* Ulysses *by James Joyce (notice it suggests we "start* Ulysses*," but doesn't require that we finish it).*
3. *(Go to your local video store and rent)* The Field, *...* In the Name of the Father, *(or* The Secret of Roan Inish *or perhaps* The Quiet Man*).*
4. *Walk in the rain.*
5. *Tell/listen to a long story.*
6. *Listen to the Pogues, early U-2, The Oyster Band, and The Saw Doctors (for those of us not in "Generation X," those are Irish rock bands).*
7. *Respect the spirits, faeries and the leprechauns that populate the earth.*
8. *Drink another pot of tea.*
9. *Wear green (in the 1790's Irishmen were imprisoned by the British for wearing green).*
10. *Laugh heartily, philosophize gently, and carry on bravely in the face of adversity.*[1]

61

To that list of wonderful things we can all do today to be more "Irish," I would add one more: "Listen to a sermon about Saint Patrick!" That's what we're going to do today! Who was Saint Patrick? I mean, really. What did he stand for? I think the life of Saint Patrick has a lot to teach us: about overcoming tragedy, about listening to God, about humility, about self-sacrifice, about finding Christ in all things. These are all good things to remember, especially during Lent. Let me then share with you the story of Saint Patrick, as I learned it.

Patrick was born, not in Ireland, but in Britain, in the early years of the Church, around 390 A.D. Britain was then considered the outermost colony of the Roman Empire, at the edge of the civilized world. Remember Hadrian's Wall, built to keep those "barbarian" Scotsmen out? Patrick himself was of noble birth. His father was a public official. His family had a villa, land, servants, and slaves and Patrick enjoyed an easy life.

That is, until he was sixteen years old, when his part of the countryside was attacked by Irish raiders. These fierce warriors sailed across the Irish Sea in animal-skin boats. When they landed they burned villages, plundered estates, and captured slaves. Along with thousands of his countrymen, Patrick was taken back to Ireland. For the next six years he was a slave, mostly herding pigs.

Now, Patrick had not been raised in an especially religious household, but during this period of suffering his faith grew stronger. In his autobiography, titled *Confession*, which he wrote late in life, he reported that he prayed "100 times a day, as many at night." Patrick continues, "Even when I was staying out in the woods or on the mountain ... used to feel no ill effect...." Patrick was developing a relationship with God through prayer, a relationship that would last the rest of his life.

At many points in his life, Patrick had visions. In his autobiography he writes that many messages came to him in dreams. For example, after he had been a slave for six years, one night in his sleep he heard a voice saying, "You have been right to fast because you will soon return to your home." Soon afterward Patrick received another message in a dream which said, "Look, your ship is ready."

62

Believing in God's promise, Patrick resolved to escape. He walked 200 miles to the coast, a runaway slave in danger at every moment of being recaptured and killed. But God kept Patrick safe and he did indeed find a ship: a very strange ship. It was departing Ireland for Britain with a cargo of dogs! The captain originally refused to have anything to do with this tattered fugitive. But the young man prayed and the captain changed his mind. But what a voyage! Escaping Ireland on a ship full of dogs!

It was an unusual homecoming. The ship struck land on a desolate part of the coast. Patrick and the crew, plus the dogs, wandered for 28 days without seeing people, finding a village, or getting a decent meal.

Patrick survived the ordeal with his faith strengthened. Now 22, he decided to become a priest. He studied, was ordained, and returned to his family in Britain where he lived in peace and happiness for about twenty years.

Then he had another one of his dreams. In the dream a man, representing the voice of the Irish, spoke to him, saying, "We pray thee, holy youth, come and walk among us once again." Patrick interpreted the dream as a call to service. He set about getting assigned to be a missionary to Ireland.

Now Patrick, mind you, was not a self-promoting sort of person. His autobiography shows us how little he thought of himself. He refers to himself as "Patrick, a sinner, most unlearned, the least of all the faithful ... utterly despised by many." Apparently his superiors weren't that impressed with Patrick either, because the assignment to preach to the Irish went to someone else. Only after the first candidate died was Patrick sent to Ireland as his superiors' second choice.

It was no small task. The Celtic people who lived in Ireland were fierce, pagan warriors. There were numerous local chieftains and a class of Druid priests that were threatened by change. Patrick returned to Ireland, where he had been a slave, at the risk of his life. At any moment the kings, the Druids, or the common people could have risen up and had him killed. Patrick writes, "Every day I expected either violent death or to be defrauded or to be reduced to slavery." But he also writes, "If I should be worthy, I am ready

63

to give even my life unhesitatingly and most joyfully for his name's sake."

Patrick did suffer. There were years of tiring work, frequent threats to his life, hunger, persecution, and even a period of imprisonment, his legs in irons. Yet patient Patrick stuck with the task.

Danger from his enemies was not his only problem. The greatest disappointment of Patrick's life was his betrayal by a friend. It seems that when Patrick was fifteen, he committed a youthful sin (he doesn't say what) for which he was repentant. Some ten or fifteen years later, before taking holy orders, he confessed that sin to his superior, another priest. Thirty years after that that same man, whom Patrick called "his dearest friend," made Patrick's confession public! Patrick was humiliated, tried, and removed from office as Bishop of Ireland. This betrayal by his friend was even worse than being a slave. But Patrick rallied and appealed his case to Rome, where the ancient sin was forgiven and his bishopric restored.

In the last thirty years of his life, Patrick Christianized most of Ireland. He himself baptized tens of thousands of people. Before his time, there were few Christians in Ireland. They were outnumbered and threatened. Since Patrick, Ireland has become one of the bulwarks of the faith. Ireland was a light to the church in the Dark Ages. British Christians used to send their sons to Ireland to get a good foundation for the Christian life. Even today, 95 percent of the population of Ireland is Roman Catholic. The Irish still have one of the highest records of church attendance of anywhere in the world. All this because a humble British Christian named Patrick accepted God's calling to bring the gospel to the same people who had made him a slave!

How could we sum up the life of Saint Patrick? There are many admirable characteristics to this man. He didn't give up in the face of suffering, danger, or betrayal. He was faithful in prayer. He responded to the guidance of God. He was humble and sincere and willing to sacrifice himself for others. He was able to forgive even when harmed.

But most of all, he was able to find Christ in all things. That's what his wonderful prayer, "Saint Patrick's Breastplate" is about,

Christ in *all* things: "Christ, be with me, Christ before me, Christ behind me, Christ in me, Christ beneath me, Christ above me, Christ on my right, Christ on my left," and so on. Patrick found something of Christ in everything, even in his suffering.

Patrick didn't have a faith that asked God to protect him from suffering. He went through too much in his life to hope for that. He was just looking for the presence of Christ in all things, *including* in suffering. Certainly Patrick could have affirmed the words of the Apostle Paul: "Suffering produces endurance, and endurance produces character, and character produces hope, and hope does not disappoint us, because God's love has been poured into our hearts through the Holy Spirit which has been given to us" (Romans 5:3-5 RSV).

"Go Neirigh An Bothar Libh, Slan Agus Vannacht" (pronounced ga nearig an bothar live, slan agus vannech). That's Irish for "May the road rise to greet you, and may God bless you." May something of Saint Patrick — his faith, his courage, his ability to find Christ in all things — go with you on your life's "journey." Who knows what *we* might do with our lives if *we* had that kind of faith?

---

1. Adapted from *Union News*, Springfield, Massachusetts, March 16, 1994.

65

Where Are The Clowns?

1 Corinthians 1:26-31

Many of us are familiar with Stephen Sondheim's wonderful musical, *A Little Night Music*, and, perhaps, especially familiar with that show's best-known song, "Send In The Clowns." "Send In The Clowns" is a haunting, poignant, powerful solo about missed opportunities, confusing relationships, and life's complexities. The refrain, at one point, goes "Send in the clowns ... Where are the clowns? There ought to be clowns."

There are many "clown" figures in the Bible. Consider, for example, the figure of Noah. In the story, Noah builds an ark described as being 45 feet high, 75 feet wide, and 450 feet long: in the middle of a desert, miles away from any water! Then he waited for rain, enough rain to float the ark. Noah's neighbors thought he was a clown.

What about the figure of Moses? Picture Moses, the ragged fugitive from justice, still brushing off the dust from the desert, standing in the courts of mighty Pharaoh and stammering out: "I met God on the side of a mountain. God spoke to me in a burning bush. God said to *me*, Go tell Pharaoh, 'Let my people go!' " Pharaoh and his advisors must have laughed.

Or, in the New Testament, there's Simon Peter. Peter was the first to profess his faith in Jesus as the Christ. But also the one who denied even knowing Jesus — three times. Peter was hotheaded, impulsive, unstable, "rocky." Yet Jesus changed his name from "Simon" to "Peter," called him "The Rock," and said, "on this Rock I will build my church" (Matthew 16, 18 RSV).

Noah, Moses, David, Peter, and many other figures in scripture: by conventional standards, their stories seem rather "foolish." Yet God chose them to be God's instruments. As Paul puts it in the lesson read today, "God chose what is foolish in the world

67

to shame the wise, God chose what is weak in the world to shame the strong, God chose what is low and despised in the world, even things that are not, to bring to nothing things that are ..." (1 Corinthians 1:27-28 RSV). When God wants something done, often God does send in the clowns. "For God's foolishness is wiser than human wisdom, and God's weakness is stronger than human strength" (v. 25 NRSV).

There was a lot of that "divine foolishness" in the life of Jesus. In fact, in the Middle Ages, Christ was often depicted in woodcuts as a jester or clown, sometimes having the head of a donkey in place of his own. There was no disrespect intended. Rather, this "Christ as Clown" image was an honest recognition that Christ's path often seems foolish compared to the ways of the world.

That's brought out in Phillips Brooks' famous piece, "One Solitary Life."

> *Here was a young man who was born in an obscure village, the child of a peasant woman. He grew up in another village. He worked in a carpenter shop until he was thirty. Then for three years he was an itinerant preacher.*
>
> *He never wrote a book. He never held an office. He never owned a home. He never had a family. He never went to college. He never put his foot inside a big city. He never traveled more than two hundred miles from the place where he was born.*
>
> *While he was still a young man, the tide of public opinion turned against him. His friends ran away. He was turned over to his enemies. He went through the mockery of a trial. He was nailed to a cross between two thieves. While he was dying, his executioners gambled for the only piece of property he had on earth, and that was his coat. When he was dead, he was laid in a borrowed grave through the pity of a friend.[1]*

By worldly standards of accomplishment and success, Jesus' life looks like a failure, like "foolishness," doesn't it?

Yet Phillips Brooks continues:

Nineteen wide centuries have come and gone, and today he is the central figure of the human race and the leader of the column of progress. All the armies that ever marched, all of the navies that ever sailed, all of the parliaments that ever sat, all of the kings that ever reigned have not affected the life of (hu)man(ity) on earth as much as this One Solitary Life.[2]

Jesus lived a kind of "holy foolishness." But God chose to use the "folly" of the cross, a scandal to the world, a stumbling block to the wise, to save and transform humankind. Holy "fools," picking up their own crosses and following in the footsteps of Christ, have been transforming the world in his name ever since.

There was Saint Francis of Assisi, giving up the wealth and privilege of his father's home to live in poverty, preaching the gospel, talking to the birds, embracing lepers. Or George Fox, the British Quaker: in and out of prison for refusing to bow to anyone but God; beaten and berated for preaching the bold message that the Light of God shines in every human being. Or Martin Luther, the lonely, middle-aged monk challenging the power structure of the worldwide church, taking on the Pope, the Vicar of Christ, standing alone before cardinals and princes to proclaim, at the risk of his life, "My conscience is captive to the Word of God. God help me. Here I stand. Amen." Also Mother Teresa, leaving the safety and security of the convent to bring in abandoned infants from the Calcutta streets and tending the wounds of dying lepers. There's Millard Fuller, founder of Habitat for Humanity, the millionaire who sold his business, gave all his money to the poor, moved to Georgia to live on a farm ... and who there was gripped by the vision of irradiating poverty housing from the face of the planet. He and his followers have built over 40,000 houses so far.

Foolishness? Maybe. But a "holy" foolishness. When God needs a job done, God often sends in the "clowns"; those who are willing to take seriously the gospel of Jesus Christ, with all its costly discipleship and all its joy.

69

I wonder if any of you have ever been to a rodeo? One of the events in most rodeos is bull riding. A rider gets on the back of a bull. The contest is to see how long he or she can stay on. It's a scary, dangerous, life-threatening sport, for riders are frequently thrown off and gored or trampled by the bulls.

When the bull, with the rider on its back, roars out of the shoot and into the corral, the clowns are always there: rodeo clowns with baggy pants and wild tufts of hair.

Oh, they were there in the corral before, of course, to amuse the crowd. Filling up time between the riders with silly antics, stumbling over their shoes, falling down, bumping into each other.

But when the rider comes into the corral, the clowns are suddenly all business, for they are there to save his life. Should he get bucked off the bull, it is the clowns who come to his rescue. Some of them distract the bull while others carry him off. If the rider's down and hurting, as often happens, the clowns will place themselves between the rider and the bull to save him.

That's something like what Jesus did for us. He became a "clown," despised by the world, rejected, humiliated, abandoned, and finally, nailed to a cross for our sake to save us from sin. The clown became the crucified, and, also, the "Resurrected One." For God would not let that kind of self-sacrificing love be killed. There are crosses for God's holy "fools." But beyond the cross, whatever that might be, the promise of new life.

Maybe God looks down on his creation and says, "Where are the clowns?" Where are those who will risk loving others enough to risk and suffer something for them? There have been "clowns" in the past. We need more today. Where are the clowns? Send in the clowns! Well, maybe, just maybe, they're here.

---

1. Phillips Brooks, 1835-1893, "One Solitary Life," in the public domain and available on many websites. <www.netchct.net>

2. *Ibid.*

The Feast Of Fools

1 Corinthians 1:18-31

It's April 1, April Fool's Day. But *where* did this strange little "holiday" come from? It started in France in the fifteen hundreds. Back then the New Year used to begin on April 1. New Year's was celebrated much as we celebrate it today: with parties and dancing and overindulgence.

But in 1562, Pope Gregory introduced a new Christian calendar. The new year then began on January 1. However, just as some folks resent Daylight Savings time, some sixteenth-century Frenchmen resented and resisted the new calendar. They insisted on celebrating the New Year on April 1 as they had. Some of their more "enlightened" countrymen called them "April fools" and played little tricks on them on April first. One trick, by the way, which still continues in France today, is to stick a fake fish on an unknowing person's back. The next one who sees it will shout: "Poisson d'Avril!" ("April Fish!"). The April Fool's Day custom (minus the "April Fish") was carried to the United States.

Today, April Fool's Day often engenders silly pranks: putting salt in the sugar bowl, ripping a piece of cloth when someone bends over so it sounds like he's split his pants, pouring buckets of water under a car, then telling the owner her radiator is leaking.

April foolishness! Fun, but what does it have to do with the good news of the gospel? Maybe this: that there was a lot of "divine foolishness" in the life of Jesus the Christ.

By conventional standards, Jesus' life looks like a failure, doesn't it? After all, he went from being acclaimed by the crowds on Palm Sunday to being tried and convicted, abandoned by his closest followers, and crucified as a criminal on Good Friday — all within less than a week. So, wouldn't it be foolish to call him "Lord" and follow him? Yet, as noted church historian Kenneth

71

LaTourette reminds us, "No life ever lived on this planet has been so influential in the affairs of man as that of Christ. From that brief life, and its apparent frustration, has flowed a more powerful force for the triumphal waging of man's long battle than any other known by the human race." Because Jesus lived, "millions have had their inner conflicts resolved ... hundreds of millions have been lifted from illiteracy and ignorance" and millions have been emancipated from slavery and millions of others from enslavement to vice.[1] Jesus did live a kind of "holy foolishness," didn't he? But the mystery we proclaim is that God chose the "foolishness" of the cross, a "scandal" to Jews and a "stumbling block" to Gentiles; God chose the "foolish," "scandalous" cross to be the instrument to save and transform the world.

That's what Jesus did for you and me. He became "foolish," a "clown" (in fact, in the Middle Ages, Christ was often depicted *as* a clown), despised by the world, betrayed, rejected, humiliated, unjustly tried, abandoned — and finally, crucified. And he did it all for our sake, to save us from sin. The gospel proclaims Jesus died the death you and I deserve.

What response can you and I make to God's self-sacrifice? Hopefully one immediate response will be gratitude.

Winston Churchill said of the RAF in the Battle of Britain, "Never in the field of human conflict was so much owed by so many to so few." At Bastogne in Belguim, where American troops stubbornly held out in the Battle of the Bulge, there is a monument with an inscription. The inscription reads, "Seldom has so much American blood been shed in the course of a single action." It continues, "O Lord, help us to remember."

We are rightly thankful to the flyboys of Britain — and to the Battling (Boys) of Bastogne. But how much more do you and I owe to Christ? So, when we survey the wondrous cross, can we do it with an attitude of gratitude? For God's "foolishness" has saved those who believe from sin and death.

But can we not only be thankful to God, but also committed? Because God has not only given the good news of the gospel to us for *our* sake; God also has given *us* the Good News to live and share.

72

Are we willing to be God's "holy fools"? Will we turn the other cheek and go the second mile? Will we love our enemies and seek not to hurt them but to help them? Will we bless those who persecute us, and not curse (Matthew 5:38-44)? Will we feed the hungry, give drink to the thirsty, welcome the stranger, clothe the naked, and visit the sick and the prisoner (Matthew 25:37-39) — either personally or by supporting agencies or our church? Will we take the narrow road of high ethical standards (Matthew 7:12, 14)? Will we willingly take up a cross daily to follow Jesus Christ (Matthew 10:38)?

A few years back, Erma Bombeck said at a college commencement, "Never confuse fame and success. Madonna is one. Mother Teresa is the other." Following Jesus will not necessarily lead to fame. But God's "Holy Fools" are successful *in God's eyes*. If we are grateful for our salvation, will we commit ourselves to God's world-saving work?

Today, on April Fool's Day, we come to Christ's table, the feast of fools, because we are thankful for the "foolishness" of the gospel. Today, on April Fool's Day, we come to Christ's table, the feast of fools, because we believe "God's foolishness is wiser than human wisdom, and God's weakness is stronger than human strength" (1 Corinthians 1:25 NRSV). Today, on April Fool's Day, we come to Christ's table, the feast of fools, because we *have heard* our calling to be fools for Christ.

The humorist Mark Twain wrote, "The first of April is the day we remember what we are the other 364 days of the year." Let's hope so! For what the world needs is more "holy fools" who believe Jesus Christ is the power and wisdom of God (1 Corinthians 1:24b), and who will willingly, hopefully, and joyfully follow in his path, believing that beyond the suffering of Good Friday is the Great "April Fool's" turnaround of the Resurrection on Easter Day.

---

1. John R. W. Stott, *The Incomparable Christ* (Downer's Grove, Illinois: InterVarsity Press, 2002), p. 164.

73

(He) Put the Whole World In Our Hands

Psalm 8; Proverbs 8:1-4, 22-31

One of the *Apollo 17* astronauts said that, as he looked back upon the earth from the moon, the earth, spinning slowly against the vast, black background of space, looked like "a big, blue marble." Think about how beautiful, but fragile and precious, irreplaceable and unique, the earth is. Consider the earth.

From Psalm 8, our First Reading:

> *O Lord, our Lord, how majestic is thy name in all the earth ... When I look at thy heavens, the work of thy fingers, the moon and the stars which thou hast established; What is man that thou art mindful of him, and the son of man that thou dost care for him?*
>
> *Yet thou have made (us) little less than God, and dost crown (us) with glory and honor. Thou hast given (us) dominion (power, control, mastery) over the works of thy hands. Thou hast put all things under (our) feet. All the sheep and oxen, and also the beasts of the field, the birds of the air, and the fish of the sea, whatever passes along the paths of the sea.*
>
> *O Lord, our Lord, how majestic is thy name in all the earth!* — Psalm 8:1, 3-9 (RSV)

Think about this "big, blue marble" God has entrusted to us. It's old. Scientists estimate the earth is 4.6 billion years old. It has a solid core of iron and nickel surrounded by molten liquid. It's hot: somewhere between 1,000 and 3,000 degrees centigrade.

"O Lord, our Lord, how majestic is thy name in all the earth!"

But, at the same time, two-thirds of its surface is cooled by water: 97 percent salt water, only three percent fresh. The oceans surrounding us cover nine times the surface of the moon. The earth below our feet is, in a sense, "alive." Beneath the surface, twelve gigantic plates, some carrying continents, are constantly drifting and shifting. Sometimes they smash into each other. The earth quakes. Above us, polar jet streams, subtropical jet streams, atmospheric winds, El Nina, hurricanes with names like "Alex," "Bonnie," and "Charley" are twirling and swirling and forming.

"O Lord, our Lord, how majestic is thy name in all the earth!"

The earth reaches up to the peak of Mount Everest, 30,000 feet in the clouds, and down to the depths of the Dead Sea, 1,300 feet below sea level. This "big, blue marble" is a marvel. It has tropical rain forests and bone-dry deserts, glaciers and grasslands, inlets and islands.

"O Lord, our Lord, how majestic is thy name in all the earth!"

Everywhere, it's bursting with a variety and richness of life, like a rhododendron blossom exploding into bloom. There's so much life. Like the Samoan dwarf goby, the world's smallest fish, so tiny each weighs just 1/14,000 of an ounce. Or the giant blue whale, that can grow to 150 tons and 110 feet long. The blue whale's tongue alone may weigh three tons, as much as 35 men. There's the smallest flowering plant, a floating duckweed so tiny 25 could fit on your fingernail, and the giant Sequoias of California, over 270 feet tall, and nearly eighty feet around. Each one has enough lumber to build forty houses.

"O Lord, our Lord, how majestic is thy name in all the earth ... Thou hast put all things under (our) feet, all sheep and oxen, and also the beasts of the field, the birds of the air and the fish of the sea, whatever passes along the paths of the sea."

Remember, you and I hold the future of life on this planet in our hands. We are meant to pass it on. But what have we done to God's good earth? We know. Already, half the rain forests are gone. Over 1,000 species are on the endangered or threatened species list in America alone. Off Cape Cod, which got its name from the abundance of cod, it's a rarity to catch a cod anymore. They're mostly gone, over-fished.

Each year, our country loses two million acres a year of prime farmland to erosion. Another million acres a year are lost to building

76

houses, roads, and shopping malls. We are losing our topsoil seventeen times faster than it is replaced.

"O Lord, our Lord, how majestic is thy name in all the earth!"

More than 20,000 pesticides, including over 600 active ingredients, stuff you and I put on our gardens and lawns, are sold in America. In 1991, the EPA found 98 different pesticides, including DDT, in the groundwater of forty states. The drinking water of over ten million people is contaminated. Some of those people live right here.

"O Lord, our Lord, how majestic is thy name in all the earth!"

God put the whole world in our hands. God entrusted this planet to us. What have we done to the earth?! How do we get out of this mess?

Let's listen again to Proverbs 8, our Second Lesson:

> *Does not wisdom call, and does not understanding raise her voice? On the heights, beside the way, at the crossroads she takes her stand; beside the gates in front of the town, at the entrance to portals she cries out: "To you, O people, I call, and my cry is to all that live. O simple ones, learn prudence; acquire intelligence, you who lack it...."* — Proverbs 8:1-5 (NRSV)

The passage continues, "When (God) assigned to the sea its limit ... Then I was beside (God) like a master worker ... rejoicing before God always ... and delighting in the human race." Wisdom concludes, "And now, my children, listen to me: happy are those who keep my ways. Hear instruction and be wise ..." (vv. 29-33a NRSV).

The unknown writer of this remarkable passage says that, when God created everything, God infused every thing with wisdom. As some beloved hymns put it, "All creatures of our God and king"; "All creatures great and small"; "All things now living" shout out to us about our responsibility for sharing and caring for the earth. Wisdom calls. Are we listening to her voice?

I think our Native American brothers and sisters have listened to the wisdom of the earth far better than most of us have. Let me close by sharing a few thoughts from a Native American. This is

77

from a letter written by Chief Seattle to President Franklin Pierce. It's nearly 150 years old, but still valid today:

> *We do not own the sweet air or the sparkle on the water ... Each pine tree shining in the sun, each sandy beach, the mist hanging in the dark woods, each space, each humming bee, every part of the Earth is sacred to my people, Holy in their memory and experience. We are part of the Earth and the Earth is part of us. The fragrant flowers are our sisters. The reindeer, the horse, the great eagle are our brothers. The rocky heights, the foaming crests of waves in the river, the sap of meadow flowers, the body heat of the pony — and of human beings — all belong to the same family ...*
>
> *We know that the White Man does not understand our way of life ... He is a stranger who comes in the night and takes what he needs. The Earth is not his friend, but his enemy, and when he has conquered it, he moves on ...*
>
> *If all the animals ceased to exist, human beings would die of a great loneliness of the spirit. For whatever happens to the animals will happen soon also to human beings.*
>
> *Continue to soil your bed and one night you will suffocate in your own wastes. Humankind has not woven the web of life. We are but the thread of it. Whatever we do to the web, we do to ourselves. All things are bound together. All things connect. Whatever befalls the Earth befalls also the children of the Earth.*[1]
> — Native American wisdom — from 1855

Challenging words. But we *can* change. I *know* we can change. *Money* magazine, in the '90s, voted Nashua, New Hampshire, "The Best Place To Live" in America. Nashua was the first recipient of that honor and the only city in America to be named twice.

In the '50s and early '60s, no one who knew Nashua would have voted it America's "best place to live." That's because the Nashua River ran through the center of the city — and the Nashua River stank.

There was the pickle factory exuding vinegar fumes. There were the paper companies. There was the tannery. On a hot summer's day, the smell couldn't be described. The water was a very suspicious chemical green. No one swam, boated, or fished in the Nashua River.

In the late '60s, they began to clean the river up. Today people swim, boat, and fish in the Nashua. A recent, special edition of *National Geographic* touted its "remarkable change." *We can change.*

"O Lord, our Lord, how majestic is thy name in all the earth!... Thou hast given (us) dominion over the works of thy hands. Thou hast put all things under (our) feet."

God trusts us. God believes in us. We can cherish and honor and protect this "big, blue marble." *We can do it! If* you and I begin to listen to *and follow* the wisdom God has put into all of creation, and into all of our hearts.

---

1. Earth Day Booklet, "Selections From The Assisi Declarations And Other Documents," unpublished, 1990, p. 3.

Theology And Ecology For A Small Planet

Psalm 8; Genesis 1:26-31

I recently learned I have an "ecological footprint." You have one, too. Our ecological footprints are the relative amount of space we each take up on the earth, not based on our actual size but on how much we consume.

Think about it like this: Everything you or I consume or use has to come from somewhere. Your worship bulletin is made from paper, which comes from a tree — which, before it was cut down, required a certain space to grow. So, the paper in your bulletin represents a tiny percentage of the footprint of that tree. The cup of coffee you had this morning was made from coffee beans, which came from a coffee plant, which grew somewhere: another small space. If you're wearing an all-cotton shirt or blouse, it came from cotton growing on a plant that took up a certain amount of the world's resources.

Everything you and I consume or use — the food we eat, the clothes we wear, the house we live in, the lot it's on, the fuel we burn in our car, the electricity lighting our sanctuary right now — can be added up. The total is the demand any one of us places on the environment. That total of our individual consumption is our personal ecological footprint.[1]

There's a quick quiz to estimate your ecological footprint on the Internet. The web site is www.lead.org/leadnet/footprint/ intro.htm. It's just twelve questions — about the gas mileage your car gets, the number of miles you drive in a year, the square footage of your house, and so on. It's an interesting quiz. Perhaps some of you will try it today.

The web site carries a warning. It says, in effect, "Watch out! Knowing your impact on the environment may cause you to think!"

It made me think. The average American — you or I — requires a thirty-acre footprint to live on. Thirty acres! That's a Ponderosa of consumption! The average Canadian requires twenty acres. They live on one third less. The average Italian uses less than half as much of the earth's resources as we do, fourteen acres. The average ecological footprint worldwide is seven acres per person. But the average man or woman in India lives on the equivalent of less than two acres. So Americans, on the average, demand more than four times as much from the environment than does the average world citizen. We consume as much as fifteen people living in India. Is that fair?

There's another issue, too. According to some calculations, the amount of space human beings take up already exceeds the planet's carrying capacity. Our total demand is already larger than the resources available on earth — and there are ninety million more people every year. Rich or poor, each one adds to demands we humans make on the planet. Clearly, as we approach Earth Day, we ought to have concerns about the ecology of our small planet. For we humans are in real danger of wearing out the world.

Our environmental problems are serious. Sometimes they may seem overwhelming. Where do we begin to better protect and preserve God's good earth? I believe the place for *Christians* to start is with theology. Theology addresses our ultimate values. That includes the value you and I place on the earth.

One writer, Michael Blaine, suggests we match "deep ecology" with "deeper theology."[2] "Deep ecology" is a phrase coined about forty years ago by Arne Naess. Naess was a Norwegian philosopher, mountaineer, and Nazi resistor. For Naess, "deep ecology" meant valuing and honoring nature simply for itself, apart from whatever use nature might have for human beings.

Think about how we might think about a tree. We could see a tree simply as a useful product. I learned somewhere that an economist once calculated the value of a fifty-year-old tree planted in Manhattan.

He estimated the value of a large, mature tree in Manhattan at about $250,000. That's the price of the wood, plus the topsoil the tree's roots keep from eroding, plus the savings in air-conditioning a tree generates by cooling buildings in the summer and the savings in heating it creates by helping break the winter wind. It also figures in the harmful effects of the carbon dioxide the tree gobbles up, plus the value of the oxygen the tree pumps into the air. $250,000 a tree! "Who wants to be a millionaire?" Most homeowners on Cape Cod *are* millionaires, at least in trees!

But that's valuing a tree only as an object. That's an "I-It" relationship. But as Martin Buber might put it, we can also have an "I-Thou" relationship with a tree.[3] We can hug it, climb it, talk to it, commune with it, and value the tree simply for being another being: beautiful and worthy, precious and lovely in itself.

That's where deep ecology touches deep theology. For what *Christians* believe about God and about God's creation will have a profound impact on how we treat trees and we use or abuse the good earth. Astute observers, including mythologist Joseph Campbell and cultural historian Lynn White, Jr., have contended that Christianity itself has contributed to environmental problems.

Let me say that again: Some contend Christianity itself has contributed to environmental problems. At issue is what the Bible seems to say about humankind's relationship with the world.

In Genesis 1:28, God tells us to "Be fruitful and multiply, and fill the earth and subdue it; and have dominion over the fish of the sea and over the birds of the air and over every living thing that moves upon the earth." In Psalm 8, the Psalmist, speaking to God, says, "You have given (humankind) dominion over the works of your hands; you have put all things under their feet, all sheep and oxen, and also the beasts of the field, the birds of the air and the fish of the sea, whatever passes along the paths of the sea" (v. 6 NRSV).

"Fill the earth and subdue it." "God puts all things under our feet." Bible passages like that *have* sometimes led what some call "Domination Theology." That's the idea that, when God created humans, God gave us free reign to subdue, dominate, and conquer all living things. Since the Industrial Revolution especially, in the last 150 years, that's exactly what we've been doing, creating ever larger ecological footprints and driving into extinction millions of species.

83

However, the Bible does not say "dominate" but "have dominion" over the earth. "Dominion" can be understood as exercising a "powerful influence" or "kindly rule."[4] In Hebrew, the word for "dominion" is the wise and just rule of a good king. Like it or not, we human beings presently *do have* a powerful influence on the planet. What we need to become is more protective, more reverent, more loving and more consciously "kindly" toward the earth.

That reverence for the earth is found throughout the Bible. Listen, for example, to these verses (all from the RSV): "The earth is the Lord's and the fullness thereof" (Psalm 24:1). "Ever since the creation of the world (God's) eternal power and divine nature, invisible though they are, have been understood and seen through the things he has made" (Romans 1:20). "... ask the beasts and they will teach you; the birds of the air and they will tell you ... The plants of the earth ... and the fish of the sea will declare (God) to you" (Job 12:7-8). Jesus himself celebrated the "birds of the air" and the "lilies of the field" (Matthew 6:26, 28).

Good theology should lead to good ecology. Genesis 1 proclaims that God made the earth and God made it good. So when we pollute the air and poison the sea and drive animals into extinction, we crucify nature and sin against God. Both theology and ecology demand we turn around. We are called to love our neighbors — including the plants and animals — we are called to love our neighbors, as we love ourselves. Reverence for the earth is the beginning of a good theology and ecology for a small planet.

But beyond changing how we think, we all must make some serious changes in how we act. For God's sake and the planet's sake, you and I must reduce our ecological footprint on the earth.

Americans, on the average, waste 25 percent of the food we buy. We each generate 25 tons of waste products a year. We all know we must drive more fuel-efficient cars, and ask ourselves, "Is this trip necessary?" We all know America needs to develop alternative energy. This Earth Day can we commit ourselves — or recommit ourselves — to change?

Will life come to an end if we each make significant reductions in our consumption? Of course not! Let me offer an illustration. In the '70s, I lived in with a family in Edinburgh, Scotland, while I spent a year studying there.

At that time, many Scottish people did not own a car. In Edinburgh, they had access to good public transportation. None of the families had central heating in their homes. Some didn't even own a refrigerator. They bought their perishables at the greengrocers every day.

The Scots lived on a whole lot less than I was accustomed to. Were they unhappy? Far from it! My Scottish friends honestly seemed to get more pure enjoyment out of simple things, like taking a walk, gardening, conversation, singing, poetry, the company of friends — and a pint at the pub. Consuming more does not necessarily make us happier. Nor did consuming less seem to make my Scottish friends unhappy. As Jesus put it, "our lives do not consist of the abundance of things" (Luke 12:15).

I'm not an economist. I don't know what might happen to the world if the average American began living more like the average Scotsman. I do know that, on average, our environmental footprint would be reduced by half. And that the lilies of the field, the birds of the air and the fish of the sea and whatever passes along the paths of the sea would have a better chance at survival. If you and I live more simply, other creatures can simply live.

Let me close with a quote found on the Internet from an activist theologian, Ron Sider of Eastern Baptist Theological Seminary. Dr. Sider writes, "If ever we are to stop destroying our environment, it will be because person by person we decide, by God's grace, to turn aside from greed and materialism. It will be because we learn that joy and fulfillment come through right relationship with God, neighbor and earth, not an ever-escalating demand for more and more material consumption. Nowhere is that more possible than in local congregations that combine prayer and action, worship and analysis, deep personal love for the Creator and for the Creator's garden."

That's a good theology for a small planet. It leads to good ecology, too.

85

1. Mathis Wackernagel and William Rees, *Our Ecological Footprint* (Gabriola Island, British Columbia, Canada: New Society Publishers, 1996).

2. Stan I. LeQuire, editor, "Deep Ecology, Deeper Theology," *The Best Preaching on Earth* (Valley Forge, Pennsylvania: Judson Press, 1996), pp. 3ff.

3. Martin Buber, *I And Thou* (New York: Scribner's, 1958), pp. 58-59.

4. Jay McDaniel, *With Roots and Wings* (Maryknoll, New York: Orbis Books, 1995), p. 120.

Anger

Ephesians 4:25-32; Matthew 5:21-24

We may come to church on Mother's Day with certain expectations. For many of us, Mother's Day is a day for Hallmark Greeting cards, Helen Steiner Rice poetry, Norman Rockwell-esque family gatherings, chocolates, corsages, and watching *I Remember Momma*. It's a day for another double helping of *Chicken Soup for the Soul*. Of all the Sundays in a year, Mother's Day is probably the day we most expect a "warm fuzzy" for a sermon.

So, *why* is the topic this morning "Anger": dark, slashing *"Anger"*? Seems out of place on Mother's Day, doesn't it? Or, does it? Mothers' Day is also known as "The Festival of the Christian Home." I grew up in a Christian home. I'm a husband and the father of a teenager in a Christian home. It has been my experience that anger is sometimes expressed in Christian homes!

Sometimes that anger may be cloaked in humor, as in the late Erma Bombeck's books, like *Motherhood: The Second Oldest Profession* or *Family Ties That Bind and Gag*. There she lists classic motherhood speeches, like: "Why you cannot have a snake for a pet."

Other times family anger is subtle, as in this exchange:

> *Fifteen year-old daughter comes into the family room where the whole family is watching television, and asks:*
> *"Has anyone seen my new blue sweater?"*
>
> *Father: "You mean the one you had to have that cost me $75?"*
>
> *Younger sister: "You mean the one you won't ever let me wear?"*
>
> *Brother: "You mean the dopey one that makes you look fat?"*

87

Grandmother: "You mean the one with the disgusting plunging neckline?"
Mother: "You mean the one that's the only piece of clothing in this entire household that has to be hand-washed in cold water?"
Fifteen-year-old daughter, just looking for her blue sweater, shakes her head in disgust and leaves.

Sometimes, as we all know, anger in the home brings painful results: verbal, psychological, or physical abuse. One woman in three is seeking treatment in hospital emergency rooms is the victim of domestic violence. One woman in four in prenatal care is the victim of domestic violence. In our state, the Department of Social Services investigates about 100,000 cases of child abuse a year. Violence in the home is a growing national problem.

"To dwell above with those we love, oh, that will be a glory. But to dwell below with those we know — that's a different story!" Yes, there can be anger in Christian homes. So, how do we deal with that anger? Admitting anger exists, as we just have, is an important first step.

A second step in dealing with anger is not just admitting it, but accepting it, in us *and* in each other. Sometimes churchgoing folks — and maybe mothers especially — feel guilty about getting angry at all. So many passages in the Bible seem to speak against anger: "Put away from you all bitterness and wrath and anger and wrangling and slander, together with all malice" (Ephesians 4:31 NRSV). "If you are angry with a brother or sister, you will be liable to judgment; and if you insult a brother or sister, you will be liable to the council; and if you say, 'You fool,' you will be liable to the hell of fire" (Matthew 5:22 NRSV). Heavy stuff! Classical Roman Catholic theology labels anger one of the seven deadly sins. but *there's really nothing wrong with being angry!*

Jesus was angry many times: as when he drove the money-changers from the Temple (Matthew 21:5ff). God is depicted as being angry in the Hebrew Scriptures 375 times.

If God and Jesus get angry, there must be something divine in anger: particularly *righteous* anger. So it must be okay for us. Thomas Fuller wrote, "Anger is the human being's first emotion."

Anger continues as our companion throughout life. I once read the average woman loses her temper three times a week. The average man loses it six times, twice as much. But, women more often get angry at people, while men more often get angry at things, like flat tires, hammers.[1] Being angry is part of being human. We not only need to acknowledge our anger, but to accept it. It's an "okay," God-given, always-with-us part of who we are.

Acknowledge our anger, accept our anger: the third step in dealing with anger is to analyze our anger. Anger seems so simple, doesn't it? Dad comes home, angry with his boss and yells at Mom. Mom, angry with Dad, yells at their son. Son, angry with Mother, yells at Little Sister. Sister, angry with Brother, goes to her room, grabs the cat and throws it off the bed. Cat, angry at all human beings, bites the head off a Barbie doll. Anger seems like a simple reaction. But, it's almost always complex.

Jack Canfield, co-author of *Chicken Soup for the Soul*, talks about the many levels of anger. Anger is the emotion visible on the surface. But often, below our anger, is hurt. Mother is angry with her teenage daughter because her daughter is withdrawn and distant. That hurts Mother. Below the hurt is usually fear: Mother may feel, "My daughter is growing away from me. I'm losing her. She doesn't love me anymore." Below the anger, hurt, and fear may be remorse and regret: "She doesn't love me because I wasn't a 'good enough' Mother." Below the remorse and regret may be affection, appreciation, and even love. Often, our anger with someone is a sign of our caring. Anger seems less damning and damaging to me than cold indifference, where there's no emotional investment, and no caring.

Hurt, fear, remorse, and regret, affection and caring: Anger is only the tip of the iceberg. So, when we're angry, it's best not to explode, at least right away. Thomas Jefferson said, "If you're angry, count to ten. If you're very angry, count to one hundred." It's not the counting that counts, but taking time before reacting. Analyzing why we're angry can teach us a lot about ourselves, and also help us think more carefully about how we choose to react.

Acknowledge our anger, accept our anger, analyze our anger; and finally, release our anger safely. Anger bottled up can be very destructive. F. I. MacMillan, an author and physician, has listed 51 illnesses associated with suppressed anger. They include high blood pressure, ulcers, tension headaches, and backaches. Trying to "put a lid" on our anger is "a pressure cooker version of anger management" — stewing and simmering on the inside until something is likely to blow. When I swallow my anger my stomach keeps score," writes Rick Warren. We've got to let the anger out, but safely. Anger is a feeling to share, not a stone to be thrown.

Dr. Frank Freed, a psychologist, wrote an article on being trapped in anger! The article includes a good illustration of how one woman released her anger in a constructive way.

> *Freed calls her "Sarah." Sarah was a young twenty-something mother. She was seething because her mother had called her three times in the last two weeks, saying, "Honey, I just happened to drive by your house again and noticed the babysitter's car was still there at midnight ... I really think you shouldn't be leaving my granddaughter with a babysitter so often."*
>
> *Sarah was seething. She told her counselor that one day when her mother called her, she got so frustrated she just put down the phone and walked around the house to cool off. When she returned ten minutes later to pick up the phone, her mother was still on the line, ranting and raving. She didn't even know her daughter had not been listening.*
>
> *Freed worked with Sarah to help her acknowledge, accept, and analyze her anger. Then they developed a strategy for a loving confrontation with her mother. Sarah invited her mother to lunch. Even before the entree arrived, Sarah said, "Mom, I want our relationship to be different. I'm giving you an A for motherhood, but I would like you to graduate to the status of friend. Just be my friend." Mother started sputtering, insisting she already was her daughter's friend.*
>
> *Sarah responded that friends don't tell friends how to live their lives. She asked her mother just to be her*

90

friend and build her up. She reminded her mother how much she disliked her mother doing that to her. Sarah concluded, "Please just be my friend." Her mother understood and began to cry. They embraced and together they worked it out.[2]

Well, it's Mother's Day. We had to have at least one "warm fuzzy." Still, that doesn't discount the fact that anger is very real in families. We need to acknowledge it, we need to accept it in ourselves and each other, analyze it, and then find ways to release it safely. When we do, it's a great gift, the gift of honesty, the gift of being *real* with one another.

I think that's what Paul meant when he wrote, "Be angry but do not sin; do not let the sun go down on your anger" (Ephesians 4:26, RSV). Anger stored up becomes hostility and aggression. We need to find safe ways to release it.

Happy Mother's Day/Festival of the Christian Home.

---

1. Rick Warren, "The Encouraging Word," Sermon Series from Saddleback Valley Community Church, Orange County, California. Used by permission.

2. Dr. Frank Freed, "Trapped In My Seething Anger," a pamphlet in *Plus* magazine, September 1997.

The Motherhood Of God

Isaiah 66:10-14a; Hosea 11:1-4; Matthew 23:37-39

A wonderfully dynamic Roman Catholic nun named Sister Miriam T. Winter was not only a noted author and lecturer, but also a songwriter — an actual "singing nun" — with about a dozen popular record albums to her credit. Sometimes, while teaching her class "MT," as she liked to be called, would take out her guitar and sing some of her songs to illustrate one or another point.

One song was titled "Mystery." She said that she felt "Mystery" was the *best* name she could think of for God, because no matter how hard we try, none of us will ever be able to figure out God completely. God will always surprise us. "It's wonderful not to be able to understand God"; meaning that any god we could grasp with our human-size brains would be a distortion. Sister Winter concluded, "Any time we think *we* have God figured out, *we'd* better stop and think. (It's) God (who) has *us* figured out!"

The title of J. B. Phillips' best seller from the 1960s was *Your God Is Too Small*. Part of Phillips' point was that as soon as we *think* we've got God all figured out, we're certainly mistaken, for what we have figured out is a false god, a distortion, what Phillips calls "God-in-a-Box."

I like that; that humbling reminder that God ultimately *is* a mystery, that we *can't* put God in a box, ever. The only time we will ever completely understand God is when we meet God, after death.

However, there are many symbols and images that can help us to understand God better. For example, one of the most used images in the Old Testament is the image of God as a Rock, such as in Psalm 19:14: God is "my rock and my redeemer" (RSV). We understand that God is not really a rock, but it's helpful to be reminded that God is *like* a rock: reliable, changeless, solid, stable, and strong.

Then there's the image that Jesus used a lot: the image of God as father. What a wonderful image that is, isn't it? What a comforting revelation, that God loves us the way a good father loves his child. All the *best* things about fatherhood are implied in that image: God as creator, protector, gentle corrector, and sustainer. Still, we understand that God is not just Father, any more than God is just rock. The image of a Father God helps us understand something, but not everything, of the wonder and mystery of God.

Along with God as rock and God as Father, and all the other images of God — God as king, God as shepherd, God as light — there's *another* image of God I'd like us to think about a bit on this Sunday. It's an image of God that's sometimes ignored or overlooked. But it is found in the Bible. It's the "mothering" image of God: another beautiful way of expressing something of the complexity and mystery of God.

Now, please, please, because I want to talk a bit about the mothering aspects of God, please don't be threatened! Some people hear this and immediately leap to, "He's out to change the Lord's Prayer!" "Our Mother, who art in heaven; Hallowed be thy name!" Folks rightly don't like having one of the foundations of their faith "fiddled with" (a least without a lot of discussion). I'm *not* proposing that.

Nor am I proposing that we adopt some kind of New Age "goddess religion." Goddess worship has played little part in the Judeo-Christian tradition. It was railed against by the prophets, who warned Israel to turn their backs on the fertility cults of the surrounding nations. The early church also rejected goddess worship. They rejected the Gnostic writings that spoke of God in feminine terms.

I'm simply suggesting, on this Mother's Day, that we consider a few passages where God is described with "mothering" images. Some folks who, perhaps because of experiences growing up, have trouble with father may find these passages to be healing and helpful. Many folks may find these images useful in expanding their appreciation for the mystery of God.

A first reference to the "mothering" qualities of God is found in Isaiah, chapter 66, verse 13, where God promises to comfort the discouraged and scattered people of Israel the way a mother comforts her child. Sometimes, when we're feeling down and discouraged, only a mother's comfort will do.

How many mothers have learned the secret that often the best form of first aid for minor cuts and bruises and life's other troubles and disappointments is mother's smile or mother's kiss?

Isaiah, chapter 66, reminds us that God is *like* a mother: providing the comfort and understanding and love that all children need. Turn to *God* in your hour of discomfort and you will find that kind of "mothering" love.

A second passage in which scholars find "mothering" imagery applied to God is Hosea, chapter 11, verses 1 through 4. Here God watches over the whole nation of Israel the way a mother watches over her toddling child.

"When Israel was a child, I loved him, and out of Egypt I called my son." Now at this point the grammar switches from singular to plural, but the image remains consistent, "The more I called them, the more they ran away from me." Doesn't that sound like a little two-year-old running away from his mother?! The passage continues, "Yet it was I who taught (Israel) to walk, I took them up in my arms." That's another mothering image. The passage concludes, "I bent down to them and fed them" (vv. 1-4 RSV). The imagery here is the image of a mother training a toddling child.

As we all know, "Mom" isn't only compassion. Good mothering also involves disciplining and directing. A good mother can be the critical force in our development.

There is a story told by Stephen Glenn about a famous research scientist. This man had made several important breakthroughs in medical science. When a newspaper reporter interviewing the scientist asked this man how he came to be so creative, the scientist gave this answer: He said that his creativity came from an early experience he had had with his mother.

The scientist was two years old at the time and had tried to take a bottle of milk from the refrigerator. His grip slipped and he spilled milk all over the floor. Mom came in. But instead of getting angry, she said, "Robert, what a great and wonderful mess you have made! I have rarely seen such a huge puddle of milk!"

Then, since the mess was already made, she invited Robert to play in the milk, which he did.

Then after a bit she asked him how he would like to clean the puddle up. Would he choose to use a sponge or a towel or a mop? He chose the sponge and together they cleaned up the mess.

Then she said, "You know, what we have here is a failed experiment in how to ... carry a big bottle of milk with two tiny hands. Let's go out in the backyard and fill the bottle with water and see if you can discover a way to carry it without dropping it." He quickly learned to carry the bottle with both hands placed just under the lip. The scientist credits his mother's gentle correction in that incident as *the* moment he learned *not* to be afraid to make mistakes.[1]

Most of our early training, discipline, and correction come from mother. In this way we also have a "mothering" God, who watches over us as closely as a mother watches over her developing child, carefully trying to teach us, every day, the behaviors we need to succeed in life.

A third and final scripture for this morning comes from the words of Jesus. In Matthew, chapter 23 Jesus says that he, God, has longed to gather up the people like a mother hen gathers her chicks. Here we see the protective element of mothering. There are few things in nature more fearsome than a mother defending her child.

Sometimes that protecting and defending is subtle. Tony Campolo, noted Christian lecturer and author, and one of *Time* magazine's choices for America's ten greatest living preachers, tells the story of growing up in a congested city. His mother, worried about his safety, hired the teenaged girl who lived next door to walk him to and from school. The girl was paid 25 cents a day for her services. In the second grade, Tony Campolo came to believe he could make the trip to school alone. He bargained with his mother, promising that for just a nickel a week, he'd be extra careful. She could keep the other twenty cents. Campolo begged and pleaded and eventually his mother gave in to his proposal. For the next two years he walked four blocks each way, crossing numerous city streets and being careful never to talk with strangers.

"Years later ... I bragged about my characteristic independence ... and reminded my family of how I had been able to take care of myself even as a small boy ... It was then that my mother laughed ... 'Did you really think you were alone?' she asked. 'Every morning when you left for school, I left with you. I walked behind you all the way. When you got out of school ... in the afternoon, I was there. I always kept myself hidden. But I was there....' "[2]

Whether we acknowledge it or not, God is there for us, too, watching over us, protecting us, and in that "mothering" fashion, trying to rescue us from sin.

There *are* a few passages of scripture that talk about God in mothering images. I think they add something to our understanding of God's mystery. God's comfort of us is like a mother's comfort, God's guidance like a mother's guidance, God's protection like a mother's protection. Not only when we look at fathers but also when we look at mothers, we can see something of the wonder and mystery and goodness of God.

---

1. Jack Canfield and Mark Victor Hansen, *A 2nd Helping of Chicken Soup for the Soul* (Deerfield Beach, Florida: Health Communications, Inc., 1994), pp. 85-86, a story by Stephen Glenn.

2. Gloria Gaither, *What My Parents Did Right* (West Monroe, Louisiana: Howard Publishing, 2002), pp. 41-42.

Memorial Daze

Ecclesiasticus 44:1-15

Roll out those lazy, hazy, crazy days of summer,
Those days of soda and pretzels and beer.
Roll out those lazy, hazy, crazy days of summer,
You'll wish that summer could always be here."
— Carste/Tobias

Remember that old sing-along song from "Mitch" Miller? Summer *officially* begins on June 21. *But* wouldn't you say summer is already here by Memorial Day?

Thirty-five million Americans traveled Memorial Day weekend. Bridges and exit ramps were bumper-to-bumper — Tauruses towing trailers, pickups pulling pop-ups, dune buggies, mini-vans, and SUVs loaded with kids and labrador retrievers. As they sat waiting for traffic to move, some drivers scratched their heads and wondered how they had missed the entrances or exits or what it is that they were doing!

Right now, across America, sail boats, powerboats, jet skis, and water skiers are slicing the water. Joggers are jogging, fishermen fishing, sunbathers bathing, beachcombers combing — and merchants smiling as cash registers ring. You and I may join in the fun this afternoon: grilling hot dogs, hosting picnics, playing croquet, chasing grandchildren, going to the beach, or bicycling.

Monday night there will be another massive traffic jam as millions of travelers funnel back home. People will cut each other off. Horns will blare. Tempers will flare. Children will whine, "Are we there yet?"

Many drivers, exhausted from the long weekend, will slouch behind the wheel in a memorable Memorial Day daze. Those of us who remain at home may feel dazed, too: from the crazy drivers, the crowds, or the clean up after a house full of guests over a three-day weekend. Roll out those lazy, hazy crazy days of summer! Some may wish September already was here!

What a contrast between the way most of us celebrate Memorial Day today and the way it was envisioned. Memorial Day was initiated in 1865 by a druggist named Henry Welles. Welles lived in Waterloo, a quiet, tree-lined, lakeside village in Upstate New York.

Wells proposed to his fellow citizens that they decorate the graves of Civil War dead. Wreaths, crosses, and bouquets were made for the day. Flags flew at half-mast. Black streamers draped porches. A local general and local clergy spoke about our debt to the dead. Everyone was reminded of the horrors of war. Henry Welles called it "Decoration Day": a day of honoring and remembering. It became a national holiday within just two years.

Welles may well have been inspired in part by the Gettysburg Address given two years earlier by Abraham Lincoln. On November 19, 1863, Abe was invited to give a short speech at the dedication of a new cemetery in Gettysburg. Tens of thousands of soldiers from the North and South were buried there — together.

We all know the legends that surround that speech. How Lincoln may have been invited more or less as an afterthought. How he wrote the Gettysburg Address on the back of an envelope (actually it was on two mismatched sheets of paper). How the previous speaker, Edward Everett, considered the greatest orator of those days, spoke first for two hours.

How the next day Everett wrote Lincoln a note, saying, "I wish that I could flatter myself that I had come as near to the central idea of the occasion in two hours as you did in two minutes." "Fourscore and seven years ago, our fathers brought forth on this continent a new nation, conceived in liberty and dedicated to the proposition that all men are created equal." Lincoln's words continue to ring around the world.

Both druggist Henry Welles and President Abraham Lincoln recognized the importance of remembering — and of rededicating ourselves to the principles for which others gave their lives. Memorial Day weekend has become a blur of picnics and parties, a

100

rush of recreation. Can we return at least a part of this weekend back to the task of remembering? The apocryphal book of Ecclesiasticus puts it like this: "Let us now praise famous men" (and women) ... our fathers (and mothers) in their generations" (Ecclesiasticus 44:1 RSV). The writer includes a moving list of many to be remembered, including not only the rich and powerful but also the peaceful and merciful.

Can you and I find time this weekend for an attitude of gratitude for others' sacrifice? We enjoy a lot of freedom in this country, don't we? Sometimes maybe too much. Unlike Kosovars, Serbians, Congolese, Ethiopians, Eritreans, Palestinians, and Israelis, most Americans can go to sleep secure at night. Most of us have plenty of possessions and plenty to eat — sometimes too much.

Can we be grateful for what Tom Brokaw calls "The Greatest Generation"? In his recent best seller, *The Greatest Generation*, Brokaw writes this about people my parents' age:

> *These men and women came of age in the Great Depression, when economic despair hovered over the land like a plague ... (J)ust as there was a glimmer of economic recovery, war exploded across Europe and Asia. When Pearl Harbor made it irrefutably clear that America was not a fortress, this generation was summoned to the parade ground and told to train for war....*[1]

As Franklin Delano Roosevelt put it, "This generation of Americans (had) a rendezvous with destiny." We are here in peace and prosperity because of other men and women's sacrifice. Can we find time this weekend for remembering — with an attitude of gratitude — what they have done for us?

Can you and I find time this weekend for rededication? That's part of what Lincoln called for in the Gettysburg Address: "That we ... highly resolve" to live in such a way "that these dead should not have died in vain."

In the 1830s, historian Alexis de Tocqueville toured America. When he returned to his native France, de Tocqueville published his observations of our country. One thing de Tocqueville wrote was, "America is great because America is good." He continued, "If America ever ceases to be good, America will cease to be great."

De Tocqueville was right. Ultimately, the security and survival of this nation rest not upon its military might but on the moral fiber of its citizens — people like you and me. Without an internal "goodness" even the greatest Superpower will fall.

Take ancient Rome. In 1787, Edward Gibbon published *The Decline and Fall of the Roman Empire.* Gibbon listed numerous reasons for Rome's fall. They included the rapid increase of divorce, undermining the family, higher and higher taxes with public monies going for bread and circuses, a mad craze for pleasure, with sports becoming more and more brutal, building gigantic armaments when the real enemy was within, and the decay of religion.[2]

Sound familiar? Sounds to me a lot like America today! Of course, no *one factor* alone, like an increase of divorce, or excessive dependence on weapons, will bring down America. But lots of them together — and to my mind *especially* the collapse of our religious underpinnings — *will create* an internal weakness that could lead to eventual collapse. When America ceases to be good, then America will cease to be great.

Memorial Day is a day for remembering and for rededication. Will you and I live in our time in such a way that we help keep America good so America can remain great?

I'm going to rewrite parts of the Gettysburg Address this morning (with apologies to Abraham Lincoln). Let's update it a bit so Lincoln's words speak more directly to us today:

> *Eleven score and three years ago our fathers and mothers brought forth on this continent a new nation, conceived in liberty and dedicated to the proposition that all people are created equal. You and I are engaged in a continuing struggle to see if any nation so conceived and so dedicated can endure. We are met on Memorial Day weekend to remember those who risked their lives or gave their lives so this nation might live.*
>
> *It is for us the living to be dedicated to the unfinished work, which they so nobly advanced. It is for us*

102

the living to be dedicated to the great task remaining before us — that these dead shall not have died in vain ... that this nation, under God, shall have a new birth of freedom — freedom not from sacrifice and service but for sacrifice and service, freedom within responsibility — so that government of the people, by the people, and for the people, shall not perish from the earth.

If this weekend brings remembering *and* rededication, then our Memorial Days will be more than just a memorable daze.

---

1. Tom Brokaw, *The Greatest Generation* (New York: Random Harvest, 1998), p. xix.

2. Edward Gibbon, *The Decline and Fall of the Roman Empire* (New York: Harper and Brothers, 1880).

Good Grief

John 11:17-36

Franklin Pierce seemed to have a lot of promise. He was bright, a Bowdoin College graduate. He was a gifted speaker. He had a commanding presence. He was pious, charming, and honest. Everyone predicted Franklin Pierce would make a great fourteenth President of the United States. Few presidents, however, have failed more dismally than Pierce.

To a large extent his failure was the result of unresolved grief. All of the Pierce's three children died young — not that unusual in the early 1800s. But their last child, Benny, died in a particularly tragic manner. Just two months before Pierce's inauguration, Benny was killed in a minor train accident.

Franklin and Jane Pierce were devastated by their loss. When they arrived in Washington a few weeks later, they asked that the traditional inaugural festivities not be held. Jane Pierce dressed only in black for the next four years. For two years she didn't leave the White House's upper rooms, her state functions being fulfilled by an aunt. Franklin, uncharacteristically, began to drink heavily. His presidency suffered.

He became the first president in American history who wanted a second term who wasn't nominated by his party for a second term. Franklin and Jane Pierce returned to Concord, New Hampshire. They attended worship every week. They held family prayers every day. Still, their grief overwhelmed them. Franklin Pierce ended up a political and social outcast, even in New Hampshire. Grief destroyed the presidency of Franklin Pierce.

What is grief?

"Grief is a young widow trying to raise her three children, alone."

105

"Grief is the man so filled with shocked uncertainty and confusion that he strikes out at the nearest person."

"Grief is a mother walking daily to a nearby cemetery to stand quietly and alone for a few minutes before going about the task of the day."

"Grief is the silent, knife-like terror and sadness that comes 100 times a day, when you start to speak to someone who is no longer there."

"Grief is the emptiness that comes when you eat alone after eating with another for many years."

"Grief is teaching yourself to go to bed without saying good night to the one who has died."

"Grief is the helpless wishing that things were different when you know they (can't be)."

"Grief is a whole cluster of adjustments, apprehensions, and uncertainties that strike life ... and make it difficult to redirect the energies of life." That's a quote from Edgar Jackson, a noted expert on grief, found in a book edited by Earl Grollman.[1]

Grief is my general topic for this morning. Grief most often comes after the death of a loved one. But it can come in many other ways, too. People can grieve the breakup of their marriage. College students can experience grief on moving away from home. We can grieve over a change in our job or over a decline in our ability or our health. All life involves loss, starting with birth, when we lose that special, biological bond we had with our mother. We lose, and grieve, and start again, our whole lives long.

But I'm convinced that there are more helpful and less helpful ways of grieving. What I would want for you, and for myself, is an experience of grief that is "good." That's not an experience of grief that is painless, effortless, or easy. Grief, by its very nature, is often discomforting, distressing, and hard. But rather, an experience of grief that does no permanent damage; that allows us to affirm life again without lasting emotional scars. "Good grief," that's what I'd like to talk about today.

It's difficult to generalize about grief. Everyone's grief is different, just like everyone's fingerprints are different. Grief work is not so much a continuous line — going from one thing to another

106

— as it is a spiral: going up a bit and then sliding back — but hopefully, always, in the end, going up.

Still, experts tell us that there are at least four important stages in grief. One important stage in "good grief" is *recognition*: acknowledging that the loss we feel is real and that it hurts.

Grief can be physically and emotionally painful. Grief can be a stress to our health. There could be a dry, cottony feeling in the throat and a tightness in the chest. Often people in grief have trouble sleeping. Widows and widowers are prone to becoming ill, especially within the first six months of their loss. There can be other physical effects.

On a psychological level, there may be confusion, numbness, unreality. Someone once wrote, "Grief is it's own anesthesia." We may find it difficult to talk, reason, or remember.

When we lose a loved one, we may feel guilty. We may be plagued by the ways we have let them down — or angry: with a doctor, a relative, the funeral director, the clergy, God, or the person who has died. *Recognition* of the power of these reactions is a first step in good grief.

A second step is *release*: allowing all those thoughts and hurt feelings to come out. A poet once wrote, "Grief is itself a medicine." Full expression of grief has a cleansing effect.

Tears are a good release of emotional tension. Washington Irving wrote, "There is a sacredness in tears. (Tears) are not the mark of weakness, but of power. (Tears) speak more eloquently than 10,000 tongues. They are messengers of overwhelming grief, of deep contrition, and of unspeakable love."

C. Charles Bachmann, a psychologist, calls tears "the best (form of) mental health insurance." He continues, "A general and genuine fear of the grief sufferer is that he will become mentally ill and suffer a nervous breakdown ... if he gives way to grief. Precisely the opposite is true."[2]

The Gospel of John tells us that when his friend, Lazarus, died, Jesus wept profusely. The Greek words we translate as "Jesus wept" are actually much stronger. They indicate Jesus was shaken by huge sobs and wracked with pain as he considered his friend's death and the pain of the two sisters, Mary and Martha.

107

"*Review*" is a third stage in "good grieving." In the case of the death of a loved one, review means learning to live with our images and memories of the deceased. Paula D'Arcy quotes W. Graham Scroggie:

> *Let grief do its work. Tramp every inch of the sorrowful way. Drink every drop of the bitter cup. Draw from memory ... (Seeing) the things our loved ones have left behind will give us daily pain — the clothes they wore, the letters they wrote, the books they read, the chairs in which they sat, the music they loved, the hymns they sang, the walks they took, the games they played, their seat in church, and much besides — but, what would we be without these reminders?*[3]

Through reviewing memories, we learn to live with the mental image of our loved one, and learn to cherish it without being obsessed by it.

Retelling our story, sometimes, over and over, is another helpful way of reviewing our loss. Paula D'Arcy writes, "Bereaved people do not tell their stories in order to *inform* listeners; they repeat the facts in order to *believe it themselves.* When they speak, it is a form of therapy ... The repetitions serve to break up the pain into smaller pieces, to make them manageable."[4] Review of memories and repetition of our story are a part of "good grief."

A final stage in "good grieving" is *return.* Return to engagement with life; reaffirmation of the basic goodness of life, in spite of its loss and pain. A rabbi writes, "the melody that the loved one played upon the piano of your life will never be played quite that way again, but we must not close the keyboard and allow the instrument to gather dust. We must seek out other artists of the spirit, new friends who gradually will help us to find the road to life again, who will walk that road with us."[5]

There is business to attend to; there are decisions to be made, new patterns to establish, and new relationships to forge. Return can take a long time, sometimes years. But it can happen. When it happens, for short periods of time, we begin to notice that the clouds are a little less dark and the sun occasionally shines. Healing and

108

reengagement with life begins again. As Madeline L'Engle has put it, "Grief doesn't leave you. You leave grief."

Recognition, release, review, and return are four stages in good grieving. They can be followed by anyone: Christian or non-Christian, atheist or believer. But our Christian faith has something additional, unique, wonderful to add: hope. Hope in God. Hope in that same power that raised Christ from the grave is at work in our lives too, in the lives of those we love and have lost, for a time.

We who believe have the promise of Easter; a promise that death is not the end of life; that the separation we experience now will not last forever; that the death of our loved one is but a temporary loss; that a glorious reunion is ahead of us, in Christ; that there will come a time that those who mourn will receive their comfort, and all sorrows will be ended, and all tears will be wiped away.

Jesus said, "I am the resurrection and the life. Those who believe in me, even though they die, will live, and everyone who lives and believes in me will never die. Do you believe this?" he asked Martha and Martha said, "Yes, Lord, I believe ..." (John 11:25-27a, NRSV).

1. Rabbi Earl Grollman, *Concerning Death: A Practical Guide for the Living* (Boston: Beacon Press, 1974), pp. 2-3, a quote from Edger Jackson.

2. C. Charles Bachmann, *Ministering to the Grief Sufferer* (Englewood Cliffs, New Jersey: Prentice Hall, 1964), p. 18.

3. Paula D'Arcy, *When Your Friend is Grieving* (Wheaton, Illinois: Harold Shaw Publishers, 1990), p. 13.

4. *Ibid.*, p. 31.

5. Granger Westberg, *Good Grief* (Philadelphia: Fortress Press, 1962), [Joshua L. Liebman, *Peace Of Mind*], pp. 59-60.

Help Wanted: Fathers

Ephesians 6:1-4; 1 Corinthians 13:4-8a

A few years ago Mass Mutual Life Insurance conducted a survey on Americans' views of their fathers. Respondents were asked to compare past fathers with fathers today. The results were somewhat surprising. On the whole, "Dear Old Dad," the "Father Knows Best" figure from the past, was preferred to today's father. But what was interesting was the people surveyed valued "Dear Old Dad" and today's dad for different things.

"Dear Old Dad" was seen to be better at discipline, at teaching the value of money and work, and at teaching his children to respect authority. By contrast, today's fathers ranked high in spending time playing with their children, helping them in school, and providing emotional support.

But it struck me that *all* these characteristics: discipline, teaching the value of work, money, and respect for authority, *plus* playing with children, helping them in school, and providing overall support — all these things are important.

That raised the question in my mind, "What makes a dad?" It seems to me it is easier to *become* a father (most of the time, becoming a father is no great trick); it's easier to become a father than it is to *be* one. What are the characteristics of a good father — or father figure (for not every child has a father in the home, but most children have father figures)? What makes a father, or father figure, "good"?

Together we could probably come up with a long list of "good dad" characteristics. This Father's Day, let me lift up just three. I'd like to do so by telling stories: true stories. For as Jesus, the Master Storyteller, knew so well, stories have a way of reaching us — and sometimes changing us — on a subconscious level.

111

True story number one was told by a professor at seminary. His five-year-old son became suddenly ill — very ill. They didn't know it at the time, but the little boy had Kawasaki Syndrome, a puzzling and potentially life-threatening collection of symptoms.

He hurt all over and cried constantly. His parents brought him to a hospital and stayed with him in shifts, day and night. One night, after the boy had been crying for hours, the distraught father asked his son if there was anything he could do to help him feel better.

The son asked his father to climb into the crib with him. So this Ph.D. Theological School Professor, tried. He found he couldn't fit in the crib. Instead he took his son out of the crib and rocked him in his arms.

What makes a father? Sometimes it's just being there. That's a good point for today's dad. Remember that wonderful novel, movie and play, *Life with Father*? Today it's statistically just as likely to be "life without father." For today more than half of American children will spend at least part of their childhood with *no* father in the home: more than half! Of the roughly sixteen million American children who live with their mom alone, forty percent haven't even seen their father in over a year!

Even if Dad is physically present, he may be emotionally absent. Urie Bronfronbrenner's famous Cornell University study found the average father spends about 37 seconds a day in conversation with each child. As a father myself, I wonder how much of those 37 seconds are consumed by "Don't do that!"

What makes a father? Sometimes what children need is simply a father or father figure who is *there for them*: whether or not he actually lives in the home; for a dad may divorce mom but not divorce his kids.

True story number two is about an eighteen-year-old who went off to college. He was a good student and made his parents proud. But one night, his parents got a midnight telephone call from the Dean. It seems there had been a fire in their son's dorm.

The fire raced throughout the building. The boy, realizing the danger, ran up and down the halls, waking up others and helping

112

them escape. He had probably saved the lives of several other students. But in the process he was terribly burned on his back.

Fortunately the damage wasn't permanent, but he had to spend several weeks in the hospital. Then, he took a leave of absence until he was fully well. During that period, the boy returned home. One thing that was required for his recovery was that someone scrub his back daily. The burned skin needed to come off so new skin could grow.

The scrubbing was a painful process and the boy hated it. Of course, none of his family and friends enjoyed inflicting pain. The father took up the task, week after week. It hurt him as much as it hurt his son.

Sometimes what it means to be a father is showing "Tough Love." Occasionally "Tough Love" takes the form of inflicting pain in order to foster recovery. Sometimes it's a hard, direct word of confrontation; but part of what makes a good father, or father figure, is being strong when being strong is required.

True story number three is about a teenage boy who got caught flipping quarters. Do you remember flipping nickels or quarters in high school? It's a form of small-time gambling. I won't describe how the system works, lest I tempt someone to start flipping quarters after worship! But it's a game where winner takes all. You can either win or lose big.

The teenaged boy in question had been pretty lucky, until one day, two of his classmates challenged him to a game — and he had no quarters of his own. He did have five or six dollars change left over from a purchase he had made at the local store for his father. He was expected to return the leftover change. Instead he gambled with his father's money — and lost it all!

Conscience stricken — and scared — he had to tell his father. He told his father how awful he felt and how stupid he had been. Miracle of miracles, the father, who didn't gamble himself, and who knew the meaning of "Tough Love," saw how badly his son felt — and forgave him. Miracle of miracles, he didn't even yell! There was no punishment at all!

But the father's reaction was so astonishing, so gracious, so forgiving, that the son was motivated to do the right thing and pay

113

the money back. That was the last time I ever flipped quarters with my friends or, to my recollection, gambled at all. Sometimes what makes a father is forgiveness: offering understanding and a fresh start to a youngster who has done wrong.

Being there, tough love, forgiveness: all important aspects of what makes a father. Our society ought to hang out a "Help Wanted" sign. Help Wanted: fathers and/or father figures who will be there with tough love and forgiveness for our children and youth.

Maybe those of us who seek to be that kind of father and/or father figure ought to be hanging out our own "Help Wanted" signs. Help Wanted: it's hard to get it right — the right mixture of presence and discipline and forgiveness. We want to be good fathers and/or good father figures. But it's a big job. Where do we turn for help?

Maybe a start is remembering that *God* has loved us like a good father. I don't know about you, but *I* have found, down through the decades, that God has been there for me, often with forgiveness, and just as often with tough love.

God wants to show us what makes a father. God wants to support us in being father figures or good fathers, so God has given us God's word as a guide in scripture: "... Fathers, do not provoke your children to anger, but bring them up in the discipline and instruction of the Lord" (Ephesians 6:4 NRSV).

God also has disclosed the nature and character of Christian love: "Love is patient; love is kind; love is not envious or boastful or arrogant or rude. (Love) does not insist on its own way; it is not irritable or resentful; (Love) does not rejoice in wrongdoing, but rejoices in the truth. (Love) bears all things, believes all things, hopes all things, endures all things. Love never ends ..." (1 Corinthians 13:4-8a NRSV). Let's let love be our guide.

For all of us, fathers or not, have already received that kind of love from God in Jesus. Can we provide the help our children want and need by turning to God for help — and passing it on?

Jesus did fathers — and father figures — everywhere a great honor by calling God "Father." May we provide the help our children want under the guidance and empowerment of our fathering and mothering God.

114

The Parable Of The Prodigal Parent

Luke 15:11-24

The fifteenth chapter of the Gospel of Luke is one of the best-known and best-loved passages in the entire Bible. It contains three wonderful parables that are found only in Luke: "The Parable of the Lost Coin," "The Parable of the Lost Sheep," and the parable I selected for reading on this Father's Day: commonly called "The Parable of the Prodigal Son," "The Parable of the Lost Son," or "The Parable of the Lost Sons" — for both sons, the prodigal and the elder brother, were each lost in his own way. A college student, by the way, once called this "The Parable of the Missing Mother," because no mother appears.

The main character in this parable is really the father. Jesus begins, "There was a *man* who had two sons." His focus is on the father. So some prefer to call this "The Parable of the Waiting Father" or "The Parable of the Loving Father." I'll call it "The Parable of the Prodigal Parent" today. The word "prodigal" has two meanings. The most common is "reckless" and "wasteful," as the Prodigal Son was reckless and wasteful. He blew his inheritance. But another, less common meaning for "prodigal" is more positive. It's "extravagant, generous, or profuse." One might say, for example, that someone offered them "prodigal" hospitality: profuse, generous, extravagant hospitality, well beyond what they expected. The father in this story was "prodigal" in that latter way. He offered extravagant, generous, profuse forgiveness and love to his wandering, wayward son.

Of course, the father in Jesus' story is meant to represent God. Jesus wants us to know that God is that kind of "prodigal" parent to us. What are some ways God has extended prodigal — extravagant, generous, profuse — forgiveness and love to each of us?

115

In the first place, God loves each of us enough to give us our freedom. God is not a clinging, controlling parent, but a liberating, "letting-go" parent. It's amazing how much freedom the father in the parable gave his child. Surely the father knew his son well enough and understood the temptations of big city life well enough to realize there was a pretty good chance his youngish, immature boy would get into big time trouble — which he did.

The father could have ordered his son to stay home on the farm. In the ancient Near East, fathers had that sort of power. Still, the father loved his son enough to trust him, to let him go, either to succeed or to fail on his own. God is like that with us. As someone has said, we have each been given a precious inheritance. We have keen minds. We can use them or waste them. We have wonderful bodies. We can keep them fit or abuse them. We have the gift of life itself. We can use our time wisely and productively, or waste it.

Most of us have received the gift of religious faith, very often passed on to us by our mother or father. As a matter of fact, the importance of fathers as passers on of the faith is often overlooked. We can live that faith — or not. God loves us enough and trusts us enough to give us freedom: freedom to do well, or freedom to make mistakes.

Robert Raines is a well-known United Church of Christ preacher and poet, associated with the Kirkridge Retreat Center in Pennsylvania. Raines writes in his book, *A Faithing Oak* about walking along a country road with his son. They go by a "No Trespassing" sign. The boy sees it and asks, "Dad, do you suppose anywhere in the world there is a sign that says 'Trespassing'?" Then father and son go on to play a game. They turn "No" signs in "Yes" signs. "No Trespassing" becomes "Trespassing," "Private, Keep Out" becomes "Public, Come In." "Stop" signs become "Go" signs, "No Parking" goes to "Parking," "Danger" to "Safety."[1]

By the way, there's power in turning a negative into a positive. Reminds me of the true story of the Protestant church and the Roman Catholic church in upstate New York, that were situated in such a way that their parking lots abutted. The Protestant church was much smaller, and their parking lot much smaller than the

116

Roman Catholic church's. Some of the Protestants took liberties parking on the fringes of the Roman Catholic lot and then walking over to their own sanctuary for worship. The Roman Catholics put up lots of signs that said "Parking for members of St. Joseph's Parish Only." The "No Parking" signs were ignored. So, one Sunday when the Protestants were in worship, a group of their Roman Catholic neighbors wired on a bumper sticker to the back bumper of every car in the lot. The bumper sticker was positive. It read, "Proud to be a member of St. Joseph's Parish." After that Sunday, the Protestants stopped parking in their lot!

Raines was amused at his son's train of thought, turning negatives into positives. He reflects that God is like that. God has placed a "Yes" sign, a "Go Ahead and Give it a Try" sign over most of our lives. To be sure, there are "No Trespassing" signs: "Thou shalt not murder," "Thou shalt not steal," "Thou shalt not bear false witness," "Thou shalt not commit adultery": the Ten Commandments. These are restrictions God has established for our good. Still, for the most part, God has given God's children freedom to explore and enjoy God's creation. God is "prodigal," profuse, generous, extravagant in the freedom God gives.

There's a second thing Jesus teaches us about God through this parable: God is the kind of parent who waits patiently for us to come to our senses. It has been noted that chapter fifteen of the Gospel of Luke is about lost things. But there's a lot of difference between a lost sheep and a lost coin and a lost son. As Bible scholar, William Barclay points out, the sheep got lost through sheer foolishness. The coin was not lost through any fault of its own. Someone misplaced it. The son, however, "deliberately went lost, callously turning his back on his father." But the son, unlike the sheep or the coin, also has free will and intelligence and can return on his own. The father waits patiently for him to come to his senses and come back on his own.[2]

There are consequences in life, costs for our decisions. Sometimes we may wish God would be like an indulgent parent, following after us and cleaning up after our messes. Maybe you've heard the story about the mother who wanted very much to encourage her teenage son to clean up his room. He was always leaving socks,

117

shoes, papers, food, all over his bedroom floor. She talked to him about it. She lectured him about it. She pleaded with him. It made no difference. His room was still a mess.

Finally, she decided she would clean his room herself, but charge him a quarter for each item she picked up off the floor. By the end of the week, she had picked up twenty items and gave him a bill for $5. He reached into his wallet, pulled out a $10 bill, handed it to his mother, and said, "Keep the change, Mom. You're doing a great job!"

God gives us our freedom, but God is not overindulgent. There are consequences in life, and we often reap what we sow. The prodigal son abused his freedom. He squandered his inheritance. His father didn't try to protect him from the cost of his actions. The law of consequences kicked in and he ended up feeding the pigs. That was about as low as a Jewish boy could go.

If and when we abuse our bodies, or abuse our minds, or use and abuse other people, or trespass where God has clearly put up a "No Trespassing" sign, God doesn't shield us from the consequences of our actions. God lets us experience the consequences so that we might grow. As the prodigal son grew, he eventually came to his senses.

There's one more thing in this parable. When his son came to his senses, and turned again home, his father welcomed him back unconditionally. Consider all that that prodigal father did for his repentant and returning son. The father sees him coming from far off. He runs out to embrace him. The son starts to confess. But the father stops him short. The father doesn't scold his son. He doesn't give him a lecture. There's no hint of "I told you so."

Instead, the father says to his servants, "Quick, bring him the best robe." The father was cloaking his son in honor. "Put a ring on his hand." The ring was the family crest, a welcome back into the family. Then, "Put shoes on his feet." Slaves walked barefoot. But sons wore shoes. Finally, "Kill the fatted calf." In the ancient world, there was no refrigeration, no way of preserving meat. So, living animals were selected and set aside to be fattened up for special meals. In Jesus' day the average person only ate meat about once a week — or on special occasions. Obviously, the father was planning a big, festive celebration. This should have been good news for everyone (except the fatted calf).

Did the boy really deserve that kind of reception? There will be some, like the elder brother, who would say a resounding "No!" The boy squandered his inheritance. He made a mess of family life. He upset his father. It doesn't seem fair.

But, as Jesus said, "I came not to call the righteous, but sinners" (Matthew 9:13b RSV). That's a good thing, because all of us are among the unrighteous. None of us will ever be good enough to completely please God. We are not saved by our virtue. We are saved by our faith in God, and by God's grace.

God, our Prodigal Parent, loves us enough to give us freedom to make mistakes. God, our Prodigal Parent, loves us enough to wait patiently for us to come to our senses. God accepts us back with unconditional love when we return, and lets us start over. In the world, we may be tempted to judge and punish the prodigal son or daughter. But God, the Prodigal Parent, throws a party on their return. The children and young people in our lives need that kind of love from those of us who are fathers or grandfathers or father figures. We also each need that kind of love ourselves. Let's thank God that God is a Prodigal Parent and live in such a way that God's prodigal love becomes evident in our lives.

---

1. Robert Raines, *A Faithing Oak* (New York: Crossroad Publications, 1984), p. 14.

2. William Barclay, *The Daily Study Bible*, The Gospel of Luke, Revised Edition (Philadelphia: Westminster Press, 1975), p. 214. This book was first published by The Saint Andrew Press, Edinburgh, Scotland, September 1953; second publishing, February 1956, p. 214.

Our Two Flags

Romans 13:1-7

O! say, can you see by the dawn's early light,
What so proudly we hailed at the twilight's last gleaming?
Whose broad stripes and bright stars through the perilous fight,
O'er the ramparts we watched were so gallantly streaming?

And the rockets' red glare, the bombs bursting in air,
Gave proof through the night that our flag was still there.
O! say, does that star-spangled banner yet wave,
O'er the land of the free and the home of the brave?

Every church I have ever served has had an American flag in the sanctuary. But our church — and many other churches — also display the Christian flag.

We're familiar with the American flag. We know the legend of how it was sewn by Betsy Ross per order of George Washington. We know its symbolism: fifty stars for fifty states, thirteen stripes for the thirteen colonies. They originally added a stripe for each new state. They decided to rethink that when they got to seventeen!

We know its Pledge of Allegiance. We know its protocol: raise it briskly, lower it slowly. *Never* let it touch the ground. We know a *lot* about the American flag, don't we?

But most of us know less about our second flag. So let me introduce you to the Christian flag. It actually is one of the oldest *unchanged* flags in the world. It was conceived at Brighton Chapel, Coney Island, New York, September 26, 1897, just over 100 years ago.

It was the start of church school year, Rally Sunday. I imagine a muggy, sticky, Sunday morning like this. I imagine lots of squirming children crowded into pews. There was to be an out-of-town

121

speaker. But the speaker didn't show. I imagine children getting restless, ponytails being pulled, spitballs flying. Sunday school superintendent Charles C. Overton charged in to save the day.

There was an American flag draped over the pulpit (where the speaker should have been speaking). Overton talked to the children about the symbolism of the American flag. Then in a flash it came to him: Why not a *Christian* flag? He made up the design for a Christian flag on the spot, explaining it to the children verbally as he developed it.

Quick thinking! Pretty impressive. It took Overton a whole week to present the first Christian flag to his church. It was exactly as he had described. It has never changed.

It has the same colors as the American flag: red, white, and blue, but, the cross is central instead of the stars. The white symbolizes the purity of a life lived in Christ, the blue our loyalty to Jesus, the red his shed blood.

There actually is a Pledge of Allegiance to the Christian flag: "I affirm my loyalty to the Christian flag and to our Savior whose cross it bears, one spiritual fellowship under that cross, uniting us in service and love."

There's a protocol for displaying it, too. Wherever it's displayed anywhere around the world, it's *supposed* to be displayed to the *right* of the national flag, in the place of honor.

On this Fourth of July weekend, let us remember that most of us live under *two* flags: the American flag (most of us are Americans) and the Christian flag (most of us are Christians). We owe obedience and loyalty to both, and both are worthy of respect.

For one thing, there is nothing contradictory about being patriotic *and* being a Christian. For instance, the New Testament/ Christian Scriptures encourage us to obey the state. Jesus told his disciples and us to "Render ... unto Caesar the things that are Caesar's" (Matthew 22:21a, KJV). In other words, like it or not, we have to pay taxes! In the Gospel of John, Jesus even acknowledges Pilate's authority to send him to the cross: "You would have no power over me unless it had been given you from above," Jesus says (John 19:10-11a, RSV).

122

Paul also stresses our responsibilities as citizens. Christians are to be subject to the governing authorities, he says (Romans 13:1). We are to thank God and pray for those in power, it says in 1 Timothy 2:1-2. (See also Titus 3:1 and 1 Peter 2:13-17.)

In most cases, it's okay to obey the state *and* to *love* our country. Contrary to Samuel Johnson, patriotism is *not* "the last refuge for the scoundrel." I like better the little couplet by English poet Alfred Housman: "How odd of God to choose the Jews." God, *God*, chose to use the Jews, a *particular* nation, as God's instrument for salvation. God *often* chooses nations as the instruments of God's will. So often it's no contradiction at all to love God and love the United States.

Or, for example, for an Englishman to love *his* country. Lord Palmerston was an influential nineteenth-century British statesman. Palmerston was intensely patriotic. Knowing this, a Frenchman once tried to win his favor. "If I were not a Frenchman, I should wish to be an Englishman," he said. Lord Palmerston was not impressed. "If I were not an Englishman, I should wish to be an Englishman," he sniffed.

Noted preacher Henry Ward Beecher wrote, "A thoughtful mind, when it sees a flag, sees not only a flag but the nation itself." Woodrow Wilson said, "The flag is the embodiment not of sentiment but of history. It represents the experiences of men and women, of those who do and live under that flag." Someone else said, "Persons not able to love their country are seriously handicapped." On the Fourth of July, we lift up the American flag and celebrate the nation it stands for, and that's good.

But there's that *other* flag, the Christian flag that we also live under. And *this flag* is a constant reminder, every time we worship in this sanctuary; *this flag* is a reminder of what *must* come first. Jesus *did* say, "Render ... unto Caesar the things that are Caesar's ..." — obedience to the state, respect for authority, love of country: all important! But the complete sentence was "Render unto Caesar the things that are Caesar's, and to God the things that are God's" (Matthew 22:21 KJV).

We Christians live under dual citizenship. We are citizens of our country *and* citizens of the realm, the kingdom of God. I

123

believe the *best* thing we can do for this country, the *most helpful* thing we can do for this country, is to try to understand God's will for America and to struggle to do it. Patriotism is never "Our country, right or wrong," as Stephen Decatur once said. Rather it's "Our country, right or wrong. When right, to be kept right. When wrong, to be put right," as Senator and newspaper editor Carl Schurz responded.

I think everyone would agree "Teddy" Roosevelt was a patriot; even a Super Patriot. "T. R." was the quintessential tough guy, a war hero, the president who spoke softly but carried a big stick. It was patriotism that drove him to lead his roughriders through the hail of Spanish gunfire up San Juan Hill.

But "Teddy" Roosevelt was being *just as patriotic* when he wrote: "This country will not be a good place for any of us to live in until we make it a good place for all of us to live in." This country will not be a good place for any of us to live in until we make it a good place for all of us to live in. True patriotism calls America to be as good as its promise: one nation under God with liberty and justice *for all.*

Columnist James Reston writes, "America is a nation with a conscience. Usually it's a troubled conscience because we are not living up to what we were taught we were." That troubled conscience is good. It calls Americans to keep struggling and making changes until *everyone* in this country receives the legal rights and economic security that *most* of us take for granted: regardless of age, class, race, religious background, or orientation.

"O! say, can you see by the dawn's early light." When people sing The National Anthem, they usually face the flag. Like Francis Scott Key watching the bombardment of Fort McHenry, we look for the flag in the dawn's early light.

Now we face this new millennium. How does America look in the light of that new day? As we celebrate the flag, will we notice the destruction that is around the flagpole? Will we see the pollution, staining our air, water, and land? Will we see the appalling number of homeless men, women, and children wandering aimlessly on the streets of America? Will we spot bullet holes shot

124

into our flag in our inner cities — and sometimes in our schools? Will we see our flag flying only in the service of our national self-interest? Or flying as a banner for justice, security, and peace? Do we see the flag as a sign of our independence and our rights, or a symbol of our interdependence and our responsibilities to each other?

If the light of dawn is not bright enough to reveal these flaws, it is up to the church, under the flag of Christ, to turn on the spotlight and to speak a word of accountability and warning to ourselves and to the America we love.

We live under two flags. Both are important. Both call this great nation and its citizens to live up to its promise, to be the land of the free and the home of the brave — with liberty and justice for all.

America The Beautiful

Matthew 22:15-22

O beautiful for spacious skies,
For amber waves of grain,
For purple mountain majesties,
Above the fruited plain!

A survey once discovered that "America The Beautiful" is the best-loved patriotic hymn in America: more beloved than our national anthem. In fact, Congress has been petitioned on numerous occasions to have "America The Beautiful" replace "The Star-spangled Banner." Proponents point out it's less militaristic, doesn't have a high F, and sounds better at the beginning of baseball games!

We all know this hymn well. But how much do we know about its author? For example, how many of you knew Katherine Lee Bates was born in Falmouth, Massachusetts? All right, how many of you knew that when she first published "American The Beautiful," the first line was, "O beautiful for *halcyon* skies, For amber waves of grain, For purple mountain majesties, above the *enameled* plain!" "Halcyon skies, enameled plains?!" I can just hear one of my former English professors saying, "What an *interesting* choice of adjectives, Miss Bates!"

I guess you don't know *everything* about Katherine Lee Bates! Neither do I! But I thought it might be interesting, on this Independence Sunday, to honor a great patriot and hymnist. I'd like to tell you a bit about Katherine Lee Bates — *and* about how she came to write her beloved hymn. Then I'd like to close by asking *you folks* for *your* input on what Katherine Lee Bates' vision of "America the Beautiful" has to do with America today.

Katherine Lee Bates, as I said, was born in Falmouth, Massachusetts, in 1859. Her father, William, was the son of a Congregationalist minister, who was President of Middlebury College. Her mother, Cornelia, was a Mount Holyoke graduate from a wealthy and prominent family: the Lees. Sadly, William Bates had been pastor in Falmouth for only one year when he died: just a month after their fourth, and youngest child, Katherine, was born, and a week after he baptized her.

So Katherine, called "Katie," grew up in Falmouth in genteel poverty. The Bates were well-loved and much-respected, but painfully poor. Katie herself was a sensitive child. She thought the church bell — made by Paul Revere — was speaking just to her. She wrote poetry from a very early age. Unfortunately, none of her earliest poems survive. Katie wrote poems in chalk on a slate, then erased them. The Bates were too poor to buy paper!

A big day came in 1867, when Katie was eight. Her mother gave her a whole book of paper, an 1867 "Line-a-Day" diary her mother had gotten for Christmas, but was too busy to use. She wrote her poems and thoughts in the "Line-a-Day" diary. Her dream was to write a poem that would move people, *and* be remembered after her death.

When Katie was twelve, her family moved from Falmouth to just outside of Boston, to a small town then called "Grantville." Today we call that village Wellesley Hills. They moved to care for an elderly aunt, Catherine Lee, for whom Katie had been named. It was 1871. A new college for women, Wellesley College, was just being built on the hills.

After graduating from Needham High School and doing a post-graduate year at Newton High, Katie was accepted at Wellesley. She found the studying easy, the social life stimulating — and the discipline hard. Students attended mandatory chapel twice a day, morning and evening. They also had one hour of Bible study, three hours of recitation, six hours of study hall, one hour of outdoor exercise, two silent periods of twenty minutes each for meditation, and one full hour of domestic work every day!

There were rules for everything, including the type of underwear they could wear: either silk or flannel. Nothing else was allowed. Katie couldn't afford silk. It was always flannel. Still, she did well at Wellesley and was elected class president. When she graduated in 1880, her classmates applauded, "Katie, Katie, the pride of the class of '80!" Katie smiled. She taught high school for several years, including at a brand new boarding school for young women, Dana Hall. Then Katie was called as professor of English at Wellesley. She eventually became head of the English department.

Katherine wrote "America The Beautiful" in 1893. She had been invited to teach a summer course at Colorado College. Katherine had never been to the American West. As she traveled by train, she saw the "amber waves of grain" and the "purple mountain majesty" of the Rocky Mountains. She stopped in Chicago to tour the 1893 World's Fair. The exhibits were housed in a "White City": shining by day, and lit by something new, called "electricity," by night. "Thine alabaster cities gleam," she thought.

But the poem really came together on a visit to Pike's Peak, 14,000 feet. Katherine and some fellow teachers hired a prairie wagon to take them near the top. The wagon was marked "Pike's Peak, or Bust!" The ride was rough. Near the summit, they abandoned the wagon, and journeyed on by mule.

Katherine was exhausted. But as she reached the peak of Pike's Peak, a wave of excitement and joy swept through her. The view was breathtaking. It was the self-described "high point" of her life. The first lines of her hymn came to her in a flash. She eventually submitted the poem to *The Congregationalist* magazine. It was first published on July 4, 1895. Katherine Lee Bates' childhood dream had been fulfilled. She had written a poem that would move people *and* be remembered after her death.

Katherine Lee Bates returned to Wellesley, studied at Oxford, traveled the world, and continued writing and teaching. Middlebury, Oberlin, and Wellesley honored her with honorary degrees. She never married. She had many friends. But her closest companion was a collie dog named Hamlet. Katherine died at age seventy and is buried in the Oak Grove Cemetery in Falmouth.

Her great hymn, "America The Beautiful," of course, outlives her. Katherine herself believed her hymn was popular because we Americans are idealists at heart. She felt *we* have a fundamental faith in the brotherhood and sisterhood of all people. She loved

129

America, with its amber waves of grain, purple mountains, gleaming cities, halcyon skies, enameled plains, from sea to shining sea.

She loved this country enough to *long* for it to be better. She loved America enough to long for all of us to live up to our highest ideals. That, to me, is patriotism at its best. What do you think Katherine Lee Bates' great vision of America the Beautiful might have to do with American today?

Is Work A Four-Letter Word?

Psalm 104; Genesis 1:1-5, 31

He was the owner and manager of a downtown store in Utica, New York. I'll call him Fred. Fred's life was devoted to his business. As far as I could tell, Fred's business had been good to him. However, Fred's apparent success apparently came at a cost. He spent maybe sixty or seventy hours a week at his store: ordering stock, working in the back office, supervising his clerks.

In spite of his success, Fred did not appear to me to be happy. He was significantly overweight, had high blood pressure, and a bleeding ulcer. His employees found him difficult and demanding. Most of his unhappiness seemed to me to be related to work. A novelty plaque hanging in Fred's office seemed to sum up his attitude. The plaque read, "Work is a four-letter word." For Fred, it was "Hell."

Many of us are familiar with the comic strip *Dilbert*. The main character, Dilbert, is described in an August, 1996, *Newsweek* cover story as "a mouthless engineer with a perpetually bent necktie." Dilbert is a "cubicle dweller," one of thousands of employees in a huge, nameless corporation. His "office" is a tiny, pasteboard cubicle, a "rabbit warren," nine by nine.

Dilbert's boss is a balding, not-too-bright bureaucrat whose two remaining tufts of hair point up, like the horns of the devil. His dog, Dogbert, is described by *Newsweek* as a "potato-shaped ... cheerful yet ruthless consultant, whose not-terribly secret goal is to rule the world and enslave all humans." Another character, Catbert, is "a human-resources director, who before distributing pink slips, toys with employees as if they were balls of yarn."

At Dilbert's office, long hours are spent in meetings about meeting deadlines. But the deadlines get harder and harder to meet because of the hours spent in meetings! Employees are buried under a blizzard of memos to be read, initialed, and passed on. This, followed by a second round of memos instructing the employees to ignore the first. Dilbert also might describe work with a four-letter word. In Dilbert's case, that word would be "dumb."

We are in the midst of the Labor Day weekend. Traditionally, Labor Day is time for one final fling before the fall. But Labor Day was originally set aside, in 1894, as a time to pause and reflect on the meaning of our labor. That's what I'd like us to do today. What does work mean for you? If you were to describe your work with a four-letter word, what might that be? And, how do our attitudes toward work line up with the Bible?

No matter what we do for work — full-time job, two full-time jobs, three part-time jobs, house-spouse, retired but involved in community service — no matter what we do for work, our feelings toward what we do are probably mixed. There are good days and bad days. A poll found that 87 percent of American workers polled considered their workplace a "pleasant environment." But over seventy percent of those same folks reported work-related stress.

It's interesting to me that the Bible respects and reflects our ambivalent feelings. The Bible has lots of four-letter words for work, some positive, some negative. The most negative is found in Genesis, chapter 3, verses 16-19.

The unnamed writer, called *J* by scholars, proclaims work is the *wage* of sin. Adam and Eve sin. In the Garden, living was easy. But God kicks them out, East of Eden, where living is hard. Adam must earn his bread by the sweat of his brow, tilling the soil. The ground is dry and hard and filled with weeds and thorns.

Eve must suffer childbirth's pain. That's her work. Maybe that's why we call it "labor." To the writer of Genesis 3, work is negative. Work is a punishment and painful, the wage of sin.

Paul, on the other hand, is a Type-A personality — a work-aholic, loves work and is proud to tell everyone how hard he is working (1 Corinthians 15:10). Paul traveled thousands of miles around the Mediterranean, mostly on foot, preaching and teaching, founding dozens of churches. If that weren't enough work, Paul made tents on the side!

132

Workaholic Paul condemned laziness. "If you don't work, you don't eat," proclaims Paul (see 2 Thessalonians 3:10). Paul's four-letter word for work was *must*!

The Bible says work is the wage of sin and a must. But many other passages portray work as a positive. Like, Genesis, chapter 1, the first creation story. In the story, God works six days and rests on the seventh. After every "day's" work, God looks around at what God has made and says "This is good! Creating is good! Work is good!"

There's even some hints in the Bible that, for God, work is play. I like Psalm 104, that we read responsively today. What wonderful images! In the psalmist's imagination, God stretches out the heavens like a tent, rides the wind, chases away the waters with a hand-clap of thunder, flings birds singing into the air. In God's creative work, God is having fun.

That reminds me of a little piece by Tony Campolo. Campolo writes, "How did God create daisies? I say, 'Like a child.' You throw a child up in the air or bounce him off your knee. When you sit him on the floor, the first thing the kid says is, 'Do it again!' Throw him in the air; catch him, bounce him off your knee; set him on the floor. The kid's going to yell, 'Do it again!' Do it fifty times. The fiftieth time, the kid is yelling hysterically, 'Do it again! Do it again!' "

Campolo continues, "That's how God created daisies. (God) created one daisy ... (Then) in the childlike heart of God, (God) clapped and said, 'Do it again!' (God) created daisy number two. Something within God said, 'Do it again!' (God) created daisy number three and four and five. Fifty billion, trillion daisies later, the great God of the universe is still creating with childlike excitement and joy and yelling, 'Do it again!' "[1]

G. K. Chesterton said, "I think God is the only child left in the universe, and all the rest of us have grown old and cynical because of sin." I like that. Maybe, for God, creating is play. We are all made in the image of God (Genesis 1:26). Maybe we are meant to have that same kind of playful excitement about our work.

Another four-letter word the Bible connects with work is "call" or "calling." Countless times in scripture, men and women are

133

called to specific work. God called elderly Abraham to leave his home and his father and travel to an unknown land, a promised land, that God would show him. God called Moses at the burning bush to lead God's people out of slavery. God called Deborah to be a judge and Jonah and Jeremiah to be prophets. God called Paul on the Damascus Road, and Lydia to found the first European church.

We all have a call. You may not have heard yours, yet. Or, you may be hearing it, but refusing to listen. Still, we all have a call. Not always, but often, that call is connected to our work.

So, if, on this Labor Day, you find you hate your job; if you'd rather go to the dentist for a root canal than go to work; if, at 5:00, you clear out of your workplace like the fire alarm just went off; maybe those feelings and behaviors should be a little "wake-up alarm" for you.

Maybe God is calling you to change your job. Maybe it was never a good fit for you. Maybe it was once, but things have changed. We need to ask ourselves, "Is God calling me to this work? Am I working in the right place, for the right things, with the right people?" Good questions to reflect on Labor Day.

Maybe God isn't calling you to change your job, but change yourself (which is probably just as hard, maybe even harder). Keith Miller, an Episcopalian layman turned lecturer and writer, tells of the time he worked as a manager in a large oil company. Dissatisfied with his job, Miller decided he was called to change: not his work, but his attitude toward his work.

Miller started with something simple. Every time he walked to the water cooler, he prayed for the people he passed or met there. He writes:

> *Although I didn't notice any outward difference in my own attitude, some of the love and concern I began to feel for these people must have communicated itself to them, because without my saying anything about my new intention ... people began to come into my private office and talk to me about their inner lives ... I began to see the extent of the need for Christ in the lives of "successful" people.*[2]

134

Miller's apparent calling, at least at that point in his life, was to minister to his fellow workers, while still staying at his job. Work is a call. We all are called to something. Are you called to this particular work?

Two more four-letter words connected with work, and then I'll close. Those two words are "gift" and "love." When we do our work well, whatever it is, it's an act of love. "Work is love made evident," wrote Kahil Gibran. "Do everything to the glory of God," wrote the Apostle Paul (1 Corinthians 10:31). That's how Johann Sebastian Bach used to sign all his works, in Latin, *Soli Deo Gloria* (to the sole glory of God). Bach's magnificent concerts and oratorios were his gift of love to God.

It doesn't matter what we do for work, if it's legitimate and if it's done out of love. A wise person once said, an excellent janitor is more valuable to society than a mediocre philosopher. A chambermaid, making beds in an exclusive hotel, might influence the attitude of a guest going out to make a decision of world-shaking importance. It's the same principle as the now famous "butterfly effect": a butterfly, flipping its wings in Tokyo, could set off a chain of meteorological events that results in a hurricane over Houston. We don't *know* what effect our work might have. Work done with love is our gift to each other and to God.

Work done well is also a gift to ourselves. As the late Robert K. Greenleaf put it, "Work exists for the person as much as the person exists for work." To me, that's an echo of Ecclesiastes 3:13: "All of us should eat and drink and enjoy what we have worked for. It is God's gift" (TEV).

I close this sermon not with answers, but with questions. What does your work mean to you? What four-letter word might you use to describe it: Hell, dumb, must? Or, good, play, call, gift, love? What do you think God wants of you in your work? If there's a discrepancy between what you think God wants and what you are doing, what are you going to do about it?

Good questions to ponder over Labor Day.

135

1. Tony Campolo, "If I Should Wake Before I Die," *Preaching Today Audio Series*, 1993, Tape No. 124.

2. Keith Miller, *The Edge of Adventure* (Waco, Texas: Word Books, 1974), pp. 135-136.

Don't Just Do Something, Sit There!

Luke 10:38-42

I have a story about a theophany on the "Not So Lazy River." Sound mysterious — "theophany" on the "Not So Lazy River"? Actually, the "Not So Lazy River" is an amusement at Water Wizz, a water park in Wareham, Massachusetts. A "theophany" is an experience of God. The story is about meeting God in a new way while drifting in an inner tube.

A youth fellowship group was visiting the water park. The group's leader kept looking at his watch. He must have glanced at his wrist ten times. But he wasn't wearing a wristwatch: just this waterproof bracelet that proves he paid his admission.

There he was on a beautiful August day, dressed in nothing but a bathing suit, supposed to be having fun. But he was still driven by the clock. When he realized his state of mind, he resolved to relax.

There it was: the "Not So Lazy River." The "Not So Lazy" is a big meandering oval maybe thirty feet wide and a tenth of a mile long. You get into an inner tube. Your shoulders and arms flop out at one end. Your legs and feet flop out at the other. Your backside falls through the center. The gentle flow of water circles you around endlessly. You go under bridges, through a waterfall. Fountains splash down on you. A wave pool creates gentle rapids.

You just hang out in your inner tube, slowly spun, at the mercy of the current. For a while, time stands still. The youth leader was able (at last) to appreciate the beauty around him: cool water, blue sky, bright flowers, sunlight glistening off the damp rocks, the voices of excited children.

For an hour at least, he forgot to look at his "watch." He felt God's presence, in the cool water, the blue sky, the flowers, the glistening rocks, and the happy children. It was a theophany, an experience of God. God was as much there for him in the "Not So Lazy River" as in any great cathedral ever visited.

But let's climb out of the "Not So Lazy River" and head back to the world of work. In her book, *The Overworked American*, Harvard economist Juliet Schor contends Americans are working harder and longer. Time spent at work has increased nine hours per year for the last thirty consecutive years. So the average worker now works thirty days — one full month — actually *more*, per year than she or he did in 1970. Schor notes Americans report an average of only sixteen and a half hours of leisure time per week after household chores.[1]

There generally is *less* free time for women. In 1989, sociologist Arlie Hochschild published a well-known book titled *The Second Shift*. Her studies indicate that, when you factor in childcare and household duties, working mothers work an additional fifteen hours per week more than do men.[2]

One result of overwork is a monumental sleep deficit. An estimated seventy million insomniacs pace the floor every night. According to sleep researchers, the average American gets sixty to ninety minutes less sleep per night than she or he needs for optimal health and performance.

Overworked and under-rested, we may feel stressed. Thirty percent of adults say they experience high stress daily. Over one-third find their jobs their greatest source of stress. One researcher writes, "Heart disease, hypertension, gastric problems, depression, exhaustion" are on the rise. She continues, "Americans are literally working themselves to death."[3]

The retired are not exempt from stress. Many retirees say they are so busy — volunteering, traveling, babysitting, entertaining, going to the doctor — they are so busy now they don't know how they ever found time to work! Some get caught in what Richard Morgan calls "the volunteer trap." Their "Puritan work ethic" makes them feel guilty about having free time. So they sign up for too many causes and committees. It may be worse for retired women. One woman said retirement is "half the income and twice the husband!"

138

Even our vacations may not be restful. Someone defined "vacation" as a succession of 2s: 2 weeks, which may be 2 short. Afterward you are 2 tired to 2 return 2 work and 2 broke not 2!

Twenty centuries ago Jesus addressed the problem of excessive, obsessive busyness — in that incident with Mary and Martha. Martha was a "Martha Stewart" type, the hostess with the mostest. She was a blur of activity, sweeping the guest room, turning the roast, making dessert, freshening the drinks.

Martha was trying to do the right thing. But she was worn out, exhausted, and crabby. Her younger sister, Mary, was "doing nothing," just sitting at Jesus' feet. Martha went to Jesus and complained, "Lord, do you not care that my sister has left me to do all the work...? Tell her ... to help ..." (Luke 10:40 NRSV). I'm sure Martha never expected the answer she got, "Martha, Martha, you are worried and distracted by many things; there is need of only one thing. Mary has chosen the better part ..." (Luke 10:41 NRSV).

Jesus was reminding Martha (and us) that we are "human beings" not "human doings." He was saying, "Don't just do something, sit there" — and that's okay.

We, of course, do need the "Martha" in each of us. Without our internal "Martha," little would get done. There is a story that comes to us from the sixth century. A visitor once approached the monastery of Abbot Silvanius. When the traveler saw the monks working in the fields, he chided them with scripture, "Do not labor for the bread that perishes, brothers. Mary has chosen the better part."

The abbot instructed one of the brothers to show the guest to a guestroom. Suppertime came. But no one came to the guest's room to announce it. Hours passed. The guest grew more and more hungry. Still, no one came.

Finally he went out into the hall, found the abbot, and asked, "Are the monks fasting today?"

"No," answered Abbot Silvanius, "they've all eaten."

"Why wasn't *I* notified?" asked the guest.

"Oh sir, *you* are so spiritual. We knew you do not labor for the bread that perishes. We knew you would choose the better part!" The visitor apologized (maybe hoping for a late supper!).

The abbot continued, "This is how Mary needs Martha. It is only because of Martha that Mary could receive her praise."[4]

Yes, the "Martha" in each of us *is* important. But let's not forget Mary. At that moment in her life, Mary was doing the "better" thing: just experiencing and enjoying the presence of God. Really, what is more important than that?

Recently I ran into an actual Martha who reminded me of Mary. Martha is a friend of ours from high school. I visited with her several weeks ago for the first time in almost 25 years. Martha is an intelligent, industrious person: a graduate of one of America's top colleges for women. She also has earned two master's degrees. She's worked for universities, including overseas. However, her present situation is a challenge for Martha. She's single again, has some health problems, and is unemployed.

Still, I was moved and impressed by Martha's attitude. She continues as volunteer editor for an environmental newsletter. She is deeply involved in the environmental movement and in the life of her local church. Most importantly, though between jobs, Martha has a sense of calling.

She asked God in prayer what God would have her do with this period of her life between jobs. Martha is confident God heard her prayer and answered. An interior voice told Martha her mission is to accept God's love for her — and to pass that love and acceptance on to everyone she meets. She's good at it. Talking to Martha left *me* feeling good.

So often we define ourselves by our job title, or how big a department we manage, or how hard we work, or whether or not we're the perfect hostess, don't we? But what *God* wants from us — as near as I can determine — is to love us and to have us love God and to love others in God's name. To do that, like Mary, or like my friend Martha, we have to "Take time to be holy." We have to make time to sit at Jesus' feet and listen to him.

Author Juliet Schor is right, we *are* "the overworked Americans." Our workload may not change much. But our attitude toward it can. At the RCA Building on Fifth Avenue in New York, there is a statue of Atlas. This muscular man is holding up the world. Yet, in spite of his great strength, Atlas is straining under

140

the load. But on the other side of Fifth Avenue is St. Patrick's Cathedral. In St. Patrick's is a little shrine to the boy Jesus. With no effort at all, the boy Jesus holds the world in one hand.

I don't think we are meant to be watching the clock constantly. I don't think we are meant to be Martha in that incident, obsessed with perfection. I don't think we are meant to be crushed under the weight of the world. A little note seen on a busy desk puts it well: "Dear Connie, do not feel personally, irrevocably responsible for everything. That's my job." Signed, "Love, God."

From time to time we *are* meant to take a ride on the "Not So Lazy River." From time to time our Christian work is to disengage and just enjoy the goodness of God. We are called to accept God's love for us and to pass that love and acceptance on to others.

So if you find yourself constantly glancing at your watch — even if it isn't there — or screaming at your family, as Martha did with Mary; or pacing the floor in the middle of the night, unable to sleep because of stress; or feeling like Atlas, crushed under the weight of the world; remember: "Don't just do something, sit there." It's okay to take a ride on the "Not So Lazy River." We *need* to disengage, sit at the feet of Jesus, and listen to him. I think that's a good reminder for a Labor Day weekend.

---

1. Juliet Schor, *The Overworked American* (New York: Basic Books, 1991).

2. Arlie Hochschild, *The Second Shift* (New York: Avon Books, 1989).

3. *Ibid.*, Schor, p. 11.

4. Gary W. Klingsporn, ed., *The Library of Distinctive Sermons*, Vol. 3 (Sisters, Oregon: Quasar Publishing Direct, 1996), "Martha's Feast and Mary's Portion" by Gilbert R. Friends Jones, p. 86.

What's So Grand About Grandparents?

1 Corinthians 13

The title of this sermon is: "What's So Grand About Grandparents?" Many of you already knew that today has been designated "Grandparent's Day." It's a day when we are asked to remember our grandparents and great-grandparents with gifts, greeting cards, and bouquets of flowers. "Grandparent's Day" was invented about ten years ago by — can you guess? — FTD! The florists and card and candy manufacturers of America have a way of creating these new holidays. You might remember that a few years back they designated the last Sunday of October (the Sunday closest to Halloween) as "Mother-in-Law's Day." That particular holiday has not caught on. But Grandparent's Day, it would appear, is here to stay.

Why not? There *is* something "grand" about most grandparents. Let me tell you how I'm defining "grand." Not "fine and imposing in appearance" (although that *is* one definition of "grand" which many grandparents fit). Nor "large and imposing in size," which is another definition of "grand" that some grandparents fit! When I say grandparents are "grand," I'm thinking of a third definition: "very good" or "wonderful." There are many good and wonderful things that most grandparents can and do give to children and to our society.

For one thing, many grandparents can, and do, give the gift of time. We live in a busy society, often too busy. Sometimes parents just plain don't have enough time, or more often, don't make enough time for their children. Probably fathers are more guilty of this than mothers. Urie Bronfonbrenner of Cornell University once did a revealing study on the amount of time middle-class fathers actually spend interacting with their children. First, Bronfonbrenner asked the fathers to estimate how long they spent with each child daily. The fathers estimated, on the average, forty minutes. Then researchers planted a little microphone on the lapel of each youngster in the families being studied. A tape recorder attached to the microphone kept track of the actual amount of *conversation* between father and child. The average amount of time a father spent conversing with his child was (can you guess?) 37 seconds per day! Thirty-seven seconds a day! Isn't that incredible! Probably twenty of those seconds were spent with the father saying, "Sit right in your chair!" The results of that study were sobering to me as a father. Children require an investment of time: time to fly kites together and go fishing and bake cookies. Time to listen, sometimes endlessly, to their stories and jokes. But with both parents working, as is the case now in the majority of households, or with a single parent running hard to raise a family alone, time can be a precious commodity. But *grandparents* often have time to give.

Consider this prize-winning essay. It was written by a girl in third grade. Her title was "What is a Grandmother?" But I think you'll see it applies to grandfathers as well. The little girl wrote, "Grandmothers don't have to do anything except to be there. A grandfather is a man grandmother. They drive us to the market where the pretend horse is, and have lots of quarters ready. Or if they take us for walks, they slow down past things like pretty leaves and caterpillars and they never say 'Hurry up!' They have to be very smart because they answer your questions like, 'Why do dogs chase cats?' and 'How come God isn't married?'... When they read to us, they don't skip pages. And they don't mind even if it is the same story over again. Everybody should try to have a grandmother because they're the only adults who have time."

Another little girl wrote of her grandparents, "Grandmas and grandpas have nothing to do but talk to you." Many grandparents and great-grandparents are "grand" and "great" because they often do give children the gift of time. As Richard and Helen Exley put it in their wonderful little book, *Grandmas & Grandpas*, "Grandparents fill in the gap that mothers and fathers leave out."

Also, grandparents frequently have the gift of wisdom, plain old skill and insight into living, to contribute. We live in a society that celebrates youth over age. But I think it's a loss for us to overlook the wonderful gifts that many senior citizens have to share. Grandma Moses didn't even pick up a brush until she was nearly 100. Verdi wrote his masterpiece *Ave Maria* when he was 85. Alfred Lord Tennyson wrote *Crossing the Bar* when he was eighty. Sir Christopher Wren, the great London architect, builder of St. Paul's Cathedral, was creating until age eighty. What a reservoir of skill, wisdom, and experience many seniors have.

I once read a little meditation that suggested that as we become older, we are like a person climbing a mountain. When you climb a mountain, the higher up you get, often, the more out-of-breath and tired you generally become. But also, the higher up you get, the further you can see into the distance! Grandparents often do have a wisdom, developed through years of experience, a "vision" that is not found in youth, and that is valuable to youth.

This is not to say that children aren't smart. Some children are almost too clever. Consider this story. A man, while reading his newspaper, found these six unrelated words in the "personal" ads: "Faculty, personify, sluice, toxin, vortex, and aurora." That's all the entry said. Curious, the man called the editor of the local paper to discover what the ad was about. "Oh," said the editor, with a laugh. "That ad was placed by a fourteen-year-old boy. It seems his teacher promised an *A* to the first student who could find all six words in the paper!" Clever. But not wise!

It's a fact of life that young people have to make some of the most important decisions in their lives: decisions concerning dating, drugs, college, career, marriage, church involvement; they have to make some of the most important decisions of their lives when they have the least experience to draw on. They can often benefit from the "long view," the perspective, the wisdom, that their grandparents have to offer. Sometimes a child will accept that advice and guidance more readily from his or her grandparent than they will from Mother or Father.

A third thing that makes grandparents and great-grandparents "grand" and "great" is the way so many have shared their faith with

145

their grandchildren. The "Golden Years" are often filled with golden opportunities to pass on our Christian faith to another generation.

After a funeral, some time ago, a handsome young man dressed in the uniform of a sergeant, came up to the minister and said, "After we finished reciting the Lord's Prayer, I felt like calling out, 'Grandma, you owe me a buck!' " The minister must have looked puzzled, so the sergeant explained. Apparently, one afternoon his grandmother had encouraged all her grandchildren to learn the Lord's Prayer through this simple expedient: any grandchild who came back to her knowing the Lord's Prayer by heart got a dollar bill. The children all rushed off with their Bibles, learned the Lord's Prayer, and came back for their dollar. A bit mercenary, perhaps. But effective. Twenty-five years later, that grandson remembered from whom he had learned the Lord's Prayer, and exactly when he had learned the Lord's Prayer, and how he had learned the Lord's Prayer — he remembered his grandmother's faith.

Elaine Ward, a noted author and Christian educator writes: "The memories of a class of seminarians I taught, recalling their faith journeys, were filled with grandparents: 'My grandmother told me stories from the Bible' ... 'My grandfather was a minister and I have his name plaque hanging on the door of my office' ... Yet, I never mentioned the word 'grandparent' in class."[1]

How much of your faith do you owe to your grandparents? How much has their example affected who *you* are today? For most of us, it's a lot. One great blessing grandparents can give their grandchildren is to pass on the light of their faith.

Finally, grandparents have the most precious gift of all: the gift of love. Love that is patient and kind, never jealous or boastful, never arrogant or rude; love that does not insist upon having its own way, is not irritable or resentful, love that bears all things, believes all things, hopes all things, endures all things. Love that never ends. That kind of love is described by Paul in 1 Corinthians 13. Children know when they have received that kind of love.

In his book, *Ripe Old Age*, Stephen Crotts talks about how one grandchild felt about his grandfather. These are the words of a teenage boy:

146

My grandfather is 83. He talks too loud, scratches wherever he pleases (right in front of everyone), falls asleep in restaurants ... But he also diapered me when I was a baby. He taught me how to fish, hugged me no matter how dirty I was, and loved me even when I was bad. He took me to church with him, taught me to love God and people, and one day, when grandma died, he taught me never to be ashamed to cry ... And when he dies, I'll cry. Not because the end will have come for a man who had a full and beautiful life, but because no one will ever again see that divine twinkle in his eyes.[2]

What's so grand about grandparents? Their gift of time, their gift of wisdom, their sharing of their faith and especially, their gift of love: a love that is like that of God's. Today, children, today families need all the help they can get. We're grateful for grandparents who have so much to share.

---

1. Elaine Ward, in *Church Educator* (Prescott, Arizona: Educational Ministries, Inc., September, 1995).

2. Stephen M. Crotts, *Ripe Old Age: Sermons For Growing Older In The Lord* (Lima, Ohio: CSS Publishing Company, 1982).

Good-bye, Columbus?

Psalm 19:4; Isaiah 61:1-3

In 1492, Columbus sailed the ocean blue,
Columbus sailed the ocean blue,
Columbus sailed the ocean blue,
Christopher Columbus!

So went a song most of us learned in elementary school. Maybe some of you learned its companion, "The Nina, the Pinta, the Santa Maria."

I remember celebrating Columbus as the visionary explorer who proved the world was round, when everyone else thought it was flat. I remember Columbus' courage being cited, as he kept on sailing westward even though his panicked crew was convinced they would sail off the edge of the earth, or that a sea monster would swallow their ship. I remember a school book picture showing Columbus planting a cross on the beach and claiming it for Ferdinand and Isabella. Armored soldiers stood behind him, friendly "natives" in front.

Christopher Columbus, the "Admirable Admiral," was one of my childhood heroes. He was a hero to most Americans. More places in this country are named for Columbus than for any other person, except for George Washington. Both their names are applied to our capitol, Washington, D.C. (District of Columbia).

But over the last several years, the Columbus legend has been subject to massive revision. The public has discovered that Columbus didn't discover the world was round. Greek scientists had known that for 1,800 years. Christian art, 500 years before Columbus, depicts Jesus ruling over a round earth. "As sure as we know the world is round," was an expression commonly used 250 years before Columbus.

149

Nor did Columbus discover America. Evidence indicates Japanese fishermen were off the California coast as early as 3,000 B.C.E. Leif Erickson may have been in Massachusetts 500 years before Columbus. Plus tens of millions of indigenous peoples had occupied this continent for maybe 70,000 years. Didn't they discover America first?

More serious than the question of who discovered America, is what Columbus did when he got here. I once saw a wanted poster for Christopher Columbus: "Wanted," with a drawing of Columbus underneath it, wanted for "grand theft, genocide, racism, initiating the destruction of a culture, rape, torture, and maiming of indigenous people and instigator of the Big Lie." One Native American describes Columbus thusly, "In 1492 that colonial pirate, Christopher Columbus, hopelessly lost, was discovered by the people of the Americas. Since then, we have suffered 500 years of exploitation, domination and war."

In fact, what most elementary school textbooks didn't tell us was that Columbus was involved in the robbery, enslavement, and brutalization of the native population. Robbery came through Columbus' greed for gold. One of the first things he asked the Caribbean people after landing was, "Where's the gold?" Enslavement came as he captured natives to bring them back to Spain to train them as translators. Brutality came not so much from Columbus personally, as from his men. Even though he warned them repeatedly against abusing the "Indians," Columbus was unable to stop them. Starting with his second voyage, the Spanish brought dogs with them. These were battle-hardened dogs that sometimes wore armor, dogs that were trained to attack and consume human beings. The Spanish literally "unleashed the dogs of war" on the population.

The sailors and soldiers from Columbus' ships murdered thousands of men, women, and children. So some contend we should no longer celebrate Columbus Day. Are they right? Should it be "Good-bye, Columbus?"

I believe the life of Christopher Columbus still has something to teach us. The lessons are not the same as we learned in elementary school. Still, Columbus was a towering figure. In 2000, the editors of *Life* magazine ranked him the second most influential person to have lived in the last 1,000 years: second only to Thomas Edison, and ahead of Martin Luther. Columbus leaves a legacy — good and bad — we can't ignore. Instead, we need to look at him realistically, both positively and negatively. Let's try to do that today.

What lessons do we learn from Columbus? I think he provides a good warning of the dangers of fanatical religion. Christopher Columbus was a religious fanatic. Given to mystical visions, he kept a detailed *Book of Prophecies*: His account of signs the world was coming to an end. Columbus believed he had figured the date of the Second Coming. He thought he had been selected by God to usher in Jesus' return.

Columbus found it significant his name was "Christopher," which means "Christ bearer." He thought Psalm 19, verse 4 referred to him. *He* was to bring God's Word to the ends of the earth. He thought Isaiah 61:1-3 applied to him, too. *He* was the anointed one called to "bring good news to the oppressed ... to proclaim liberty to the captives, and release to the prisoners" (Isaiah 61:1a, NRSV). Ironically, Columbus didn't free anyone, but initiated a slave trade and put Native Americans in chains.

His desire for gold wasn't completely selfish, either. Columbus wanted gold to finance a crusade to "liberate" the Holy Land from the Muslims. He was driven religiously. Unfortunately, he was driven in dangerous directions. Columbus' life provides a warning about the dangers of blind, unreflective, overly self-confident faith.

That warning continues to be pertinent. Terrorists killed over 3,000 people on September 11, believing they were acting in the name of Islam. Jewish fundamentalists build settlements on the West Bank, slowing the peace process. In America, radical Right-to-Lifers have blown up clinics and gunned down doctors, believing they are acting on behalf of God.

Irish satirist (and Anglican priest) Jonathan Swift wrote, "We have just enough religion to make us hate, but not enough to make

151

us love one another." Christopher Columbus provides a warning against the kind of fanatical religion that is so certain of its own righteousness it ignores Christ's new commandment to love (John 15:12).

A second lesson learned from Columbus is to beware of cultures in collision. Two worlds met when Columbus first encountered the indigenous peoples on the beach. We know something about Christian culture in the 1400s. It had brilliant illuminated manuscripts, rich tapestries, and soaring Gothic cathedrals. There was much to value in Christian Europe. But the Caribbean people had a culture, too.

In his log, Columbus described the natives as generous, friendly, and peaceful. He reported they were completely honest. They lived in neat, small villages. They respected the environment. Unlike the Europeans, they bathed often. Their culture was 1,500 years old. But in just five decades, the explorers wiped it out.

We live in a "Global Village" and frequently encounter other cultures. For centuries the preferred "Christian approach" was to conquer and/or convert non-Christians. Today what our Global Village demands is not conquest, but cooperation. Theologian Jay McDaniel offers an analogy of a new way Christians and people of other religions, and of no religion, must get along.[1]

McDaniel asks us to imagine a deep, wide river. On the river are many rafts. Each raft represents a world religion. There's a Jewish raft, a Christian raft, a Hindu raft, a Buddhist raft, and a raft for Muslims. Plus there are canoes. The canoes represent the religions of indigenous peoples. There are African canoes, Native American canoes, Aboriginal canoes. The river represents the earth itself. All the religions, the rafts and canoes, are trying to reach the other shore, representing wholeness. There are swimmers in the river, too: people with no religious affiliation, who are trying to make it on their own.

In previous centuries, Christians claimed our raft was the only way to cross the river. In fact, in some periods, Christians tried to sink other rafts or canoes and capture or convert other people. Other world religions sometimes took the same approach.

Today those trying to cross the river need to respect and learn from each other. Each religion has something to teach. We need to work together to clean up the river. It's polluted. Together we need to rescue the drowning; the billion or so people who are being dragged down by hunger and despair.

Christopher Columbus reminds us of colliding cultures. Jay McDaniel offers a model for cultural cooperation. Reaching the other shore with our brothers and sisters of other faiths — and people of no faith — will require a new kind of explorer with the courage of Columbus, but with a different vision for a New World: cooperation, not collision.

A final thing I am reminded of as we approach Columbus Day is that you and I can do something to help right an ancient wrong. In October, every year, the United Church of Christ receives its Neighbors in Need special offering. One third of those gifts go to aid Native Americans.

The Neighbors in Need gifts are shared with twenty UCC American Indian congregations. The gifts help these small churches pay pastors and fund missions, like feeding programs after school. The gifts also provide seminary scholarship aid for Native American students. The offering is used throughout our denomination to promote multiracial and multicultural education, especially for teenagers. It helps fund the Council for American Indian Ministries (CAIM) that works for justice. As the Neighbors in Need flier puts it, "It's about Justice!" Giving generously to Neighbors in Need is something tangible we can do immediately to support Native Americans.

Columbus Day is coming. Should we observe it? If so, how? Frankly, I can't shout, "Hail, Columbus!" with the enthusiasm I did as a kid. But there are things we can learn, both negative and positive, from Columbus. For all his shortcomings, he was a courageous explorer.

We need explorers today, too. We need men and women who will explore Jesus' call to love one another as he has loved us. We need explorers who will seek not collision but a new world of cooperation with other nations, religions, and cultures. We need

153

explorers who will strive to "do justice, love kindness, and to walk humbly with our God" (Micah 6:8 NRSV) until all God's people together can make it over to the other side.

---

1. Jay McDaniel, *With Roots and Wings* (Maryknoll, New York: Orbis Books, 1995), pp. 134-149.

Indian Givers

Psalm 95:1-7a

It started with a Pow Wow in Berkeley, California. The year was 1992: the 500th anniversary of Columbus' landing. Instead of celebrating Columbus' arrival in the Americas, organizers chose to honor the more than 100 million people who already lived in this hemisphere before any Western Europeans arrived. The city council in Berkeley voted to support the effort. Columbus Day was first changed to "Indigenous Peoples' Day" in Berkeley, California. Since that time, many municipalities and organizations have set aside the second Monday of October as a day to remember Native Americans.

Today I'd like to talk a bit about "Indian" giving. Native Americans have made significant and unrecognized gifts to American and world culture. This season seems a good time to give thanks for these gifts. Consider some of the many gifts we have received from Native Americans.

According to anthropologist Jack Weatherford in his book, *Indian Giving: How the Indians of the Americas Transformed the World,* many familiar foods were first cultivated by indigenous peoples. These foods include potatoes, sweet potatoes, corn, cranberries, tomatoes, and squash; plus sugar, chocolate, and vanilla. Weatherford estimates sixty percent of all crops in cultivation worldwide were first grown by Native Americans.[1] Isn't that amazing? As we sit down to our Sunday dinners, we should be grateful to Native Americans for the foods they developed.

They were not only great farmers, but also great pharmacists, Weatherford points out. Their close connection to the earth helped them discover the medicinal properties of plants. They made a tonic from evergreen bark that tasted awful, but was loaded with

155

vitamin C, and fought scurvy. They turned shrub bark into an astringent lotion that we today call witch hazel. They discovered wintergreen and quinine and were the first to use petroleum jelly for its soothing and healing powers. I once read indigenous people discovered the precursor of aspirin, which they extracted from tree bark. Not only many of our foods but many of our medicines come via Native Americans.

Their trails became the basis for colonial roads, some of which have grown into well-known thoroughfares, like the Mohawk Trail, and even into Interstate highways. Native Americans raised a superior variety of cotton that revolutionized cloth production in Europe, leading to textile factories and the Industrial Revolution.

Native American tribal organization directly effected the shape of American government, contends Weatherford. Thomas Paine, Benjamin Franklin, and George Washington were well acquainted with Native American confederacies. In these confederacies, individual braves elected their chief, who represented the tribe at larger councils. Five large nations were unified into a league, the League of the Iroquois. Reportedly it was Canassatego, an Iroquois chief, who first suggested that the American colonials unite their colonies in a similar manner. This eventually was written into our Constitution, which resulted in our federal style of government.

Indigenous people have made significant contributions to American and world culture. Foods, medicines, and democratic traditions are only a few. One of the great gifts they have to bestow, that non-Native Americans don't always receive, is their spiritual insights. There is much indigenous peoples can teach us about living on earth.

One important gift is a deep reverence for nature. Native American spirituality reminds us nature reveals God. Black Elk, a wise Lakota Sioux living on a Reservation in South Dakota, described his understanding of God in nature like this: "... all things are the work of the Great Spirit ... He is within all things; the trees, the grasses, the rivers, the mountains and all the four-legged animals, and the winged peoples; and even more important, we should understand that he is also above all these things and peoples."[2]

156

Doesn't that remind you a bit of the Psalm I read today? Let's listen again to verses from Psalm 95:

> *O come, let us sing to the Lord;*
>   *let us make a joyful noise to the rock of our*
>   *salvation!*
> *Let us come into his presence with thanksgiving;*
>   *let us make a joyful noise to him with songs of*
>   *praise!*
> *For the Lord is a great God,*
>   *and a great King above all gods.*
> *In his hand are the depths of the earth;*
>   *the heights of the mountains are his also ...*
> *The sea is his, for he made it,*
>   *and the dry land, which his hands have formed.*
>   — Psalm 95:1-4 (NRSV)

Notice how Black Elk and the Psalmist both celebrate a Great Spirit/God who is at the same time in nature and above nature. "The heavens are telling the glory of God" (Psalm 19:1, NRSV), and the earth, too, and all that is within them. One of the gifts of Native American spirituality is reminding us to rejoice in the beauty and wonder of the earth.

Beyond that, Native Americans remind us not only of our connections with nature but also of our call to care for nature. Humankind is not above, but alongside, other living things. Nearly 150 years ago, in 1855, Chief Seattle said prophetically:

> *Teach your children what we have taught our children, that the earth is our mother. Whatever befalls the earth befalls the children of the earth. If we spit upon the ground we spit upon ourselves ... The earth does not belong to us; we belong to the earth ... This earth is precious to God, and to harm the earth is to heap contempt on its Creator. So love it as we have loved it. Care for it as we have cared for it ... And with all your mind, with all your heart, preserve it for your children and love ... as God loves us all.*[3]

157

"The earth does not belong to us; we belong to the earth ... Love (the earth) as we have loved it." That kind of reminder is a gift.

It seems to me another gift Native Americans give is their example *of* giving. "Indian giving," as it is commonly used, is a misleading phrase. It has been said, "History is written by the winners." White Europeans won the contest for our continent. White Europeans coined the phrase "Indian giving" as a put-down. Like "Indian corn" or "Indian summer," it implied something second-rate or false.

But there is nothing second-rate about indigenous peoples' generosity. Among Native Americans one way of displaying wealth is giving things away. One tribe calls this a "pot latch" ceremony. Generous gifts are made to friends and family and also to the needy. In indigenous peoples' culture, a person's greatness is measured by what they give, not what they keep. As one Native American woman put it, "When one's heart is glad, he gives away gifts." Giving is "a way of expressing joy" — something to think about at stewardship time.

Also, indigenous people traditionally stress the importance of the group over the individual and cooperation over competition. Psychotherapist Erik Erikson writes about this in his classic, *Childhood and Society*, after studying the Sioux (ch. 3). The selfishness and self-centeredness of "White" society sometimes astonishes Native Americans. Black Elk, the Sioux wise man said:

> *I could see that the Wasichus (whites) did not care for each other the way that our people did ... They would take everything from each other if they could ... there were some who had more of everything than they could use, while crowds of people had nothing at all and many were starving.*[4]

Gifts Native Americans have to give are their concern for community and their example of giving.

Native American giving includes not only giving possessions, but also self-giving. The explorer and environmentalist John Muir reports an incident from Alaska in the late 1800s. Two tribes were at war. The fighting between the two villages had gone on all summer. Because of constant attacks, the women were unable to go the salmon streams, or to gather berries for the winter.

One chief stepped into the no-man's-land between the warring villages. He shouted a proposal. Both tribes should stop fighting and use their time to prepare for winter. The other chief responded that the peace offer wasn't fair, since his tribe had lost ten more warriors in battle than the other tribe. Only if the first tribe gave up ten men, would the score be settled and he would make peace.

"Very well," said the first chief. "You know my rank. You know that I am worth ten common men, or more. Take me and make peace." The chief was promptly shot dead and peace was established. Muir writes, "That chief literally gave himself a sacrifice for his people. He died that they might live."[5]

"He died that they might live." Does that remind you of anyone? I think of Jesus. Sometimes self-sacrifice was a part of Native American giving.

Back in 1987, the United Church of Christ, in a strongly worded resolution at General Synod Sixteen, acknowledged the church's involvement in the "disparagement and undermining of Indian culture." Too often the Native American was treated as "a child in need of direction, as a savage in need of civilizing, and as a heathen in need of salvation," the document said.

That denomination offered an apology to Native Congregations. A promise was made to seek "dialogue" and "mutual concern" and "a reconciliation that seeks to share Indian wisdom, truth and sensitivity." Many other North American denominations have made similar statements.

Let me conclude with the words of Walking Buffalo:

> *Do you know that trees talk? Well they do. They talk to each other, and they'll talk to you if you listen ... White people don't listen. They never learned to listen to the Indians, so I don't suppose they'll listen to other voices in nature. But I have learned a lot from trees.*[6]

159

We have a lot to learn from trees — and from Native Americans. Indigenous people have gifted America and our world in many ways. Their material gifts, like foods and medicines, are important. Their spiritual insights are significant. The wider church reminds us to listen. Can we take time this Columbus Day/Indigenous Peoples' Day weekend to be thankful for "Indian" giving?

1. Jack Weatherford, *Indian Giving: How the Indians of the Americas Transformed the World* (New York: Crown Publishing, Inc., 1988).

2. Joseph Epes Brown, *The Sacred Pipe* (Norman, Oklahoma: University of Oklahoma, 1982), pp. ss, 59.

3. Chief Seattle, 1855.

4. The story of "Black Elk" as told by John G. Neihardt, *Black Elk Speaks* (Norman, Oklahoma: University of Oklahoma, 1934).

5. John Muir, *Travels in Alaska* (Boston: Houghton-Mifflin Company, 1915), pp. 198-199.

6. Quoted by Vine Deloria in *God is Red: A Native View of Religion* (Golden, Colorado: North American Press, 1992), p. 104.

We Need A Good Priest — Always

Hebrews 7:23-28

The purpose of this sermon is first to present Jesus Christ as our Great High Priest, as described in the book of Hebrews; *and* second, to answer a question: *If* we're Protestant: "Why ever would we *need* a priest?"

Let's begin with some history: The Sunday before October 31 is always Reformation Sunday. On the Eve of All Saints' Day (our Halloween) in 1517, an obscure Augustinian priest and college professor named Martin Luther nailed 95 theses, 95 questions for discussion, to the door of the Wittenburg, Germany, Castle Church. In those days church doors were often used as bulletin boards. Nailing things on them was not sacrilegious.

Luther merely wanted to start an academic discussion. He didn't envision kicking off the Protestant Reformation that tore Europe apart. He didn't envision becoming what some scholars say is the third most important person to live in the last millennium. But start a religious revolution he did.

One thing Martin Luther and millions of Protestants have insisted on is "The priesthood of all believers." The idea that every one of us here this morning *is* already a priest. We *are* "a chosen race, a royal priesthood, a holy nation, God's own people," to quote 1 Peter (2:49 NRSV).

Each one of us is already someone special. Each one of us has a special calling, like a priest (whether we know it or not).

So we don't need a man in a black shirt with his collar around backward as a go-between between God and us. We can "direct dial" God. No need for a priest.

Or is there? Wouldn't it be good to have a priest, an intermediary, someone who pleads our needs to God who is *always* available? There was a wrecker service in Georgia that was available

161

23 and a half hours per day. Available 23 and a half hours: great! But no one knew when that half-hour was!

Jesus, we proclaim in the Apostles' Creed, is seated at the right hand of God and now intercedes for us (see Romans 8:33). Or as Hebrews puts it, "(Jesus) always lives to make intercession to God for (those who approach God through him)" (7:25b NRSV).

"More things are wrought by prayer than this world dreams of" (Tennyson). I have seen mighty miracles of prayer in this very church. So isn't it good to know we have a Great High Priest seated right next to God — at the right hand of God — who pleads and intercedes for us always?

What a friend we have in Jesus. He's praying that we will do the right thing, find the right words to say, find the right direction. He's praying for our health and wholeness.

Someone once said ours is a "24-7-365" God. Maybe Protestants also need a good priest who is always at prayer for us. Think about Jesus praying for *you*, pleading for you this very moment and always. Maybe that image can help us be strong when we're weak.

Wouldn't it be nice to have not only a good priest who is always available, but also a good priest who is always effective? The old Temple priests needed to make sacrifices for sin day after day. All those innocent animals lined up to be slaughtered, all that innocent blood shed, day after day, year after year, century after century: and still no lasting salvation from sin. That's depressing.

Then Jesus, the spotless Lamb of God, unblemished, at once the perfect priest and the perfect sacrifice, laid down his life for our sake on the altar of the cross. As Hebrews puts it, "once for all" Jesus "offered himself for us" (7:27c NRSV).

Jesus made us right with God, "once for all." And all you have to do to be saved is to believe that. That's another of the great proclamations of the Protestant church: we are saved through faith in Jesus Christ alone.

Rediscovering that principle kept our friend Martin Luther from going crazy. Most of us know how, as an Augustinian priest, Luther fasted longer, and prayed harder, and confessed more often than did all his other brothers.

162

Martin Luther sacrificed more and more. But still he couldn't find peace for his troubled heart. Until finally he realized that it wasn't *his* sacrifices but *Christ's* sacrifice on the cross that saves, "once for all." The pent-up power of Martin Luther's revelation, once released, fired up a Reformation that changed the world.

And "once for all" comforted another great German Protestant, Dietrich Bonhoeffer. During the Second World War the Nazis threw Bonhoeffer into Finkenwalde Concentration Camp. There, in that hellhole of ugliness and death, Dietrich Bonhoeffer created a small seminary. He resisted the Nazis by teaching theology.

On the altar table where they worshiped daily was a cross with a single word engraved on it. The word on the cross was "once." "Once for all" Jesus died for your sins and my sins and for the sins of the whole world: yes, even for the sins of Adolf Hitler and the Nazis.

No need to beat ourselves constantly for our sins, no need to try to buy God's favor. Only one thing is necessary: faith in the death and resurrection of Jesus Christ.

An idealistic young man once asked a pastor how to live a holy life. The pastor told him to bicycle 25 miles a day, fast every Friday, bathe in olive oil monthly, and read the Bible through every year.

The young man tried this for two years. Then he got tired and went back to the pastor. He complained, "I bicycled, fasted, bathed, and read through the Bible. When I read the Bible the second time I realized I'm saved by faith alone. All that other stuff wasn't necessary. Why didn't you just tell me?"

To which the pastor responded, "Son, two years ago you would never have believed me if I told you how simple it was!"

We *have* a Great High Priest who *made* the right sacrifice, once for all. Believing in Jesus Christ crucified and risen is the key to salvation. Maybe Protestants *do* need a good priest who is always effective.

And I know *I* could use a good priest who always understands me. Earlier in Hebrews there are these comforting words, "For we do not have a high priest who is unable to sympathize with our weaknesses, but we have one who in every respect has been tested

163

as we are, yet without sin" (5:15 NRSV). It helps *me* to know that, in the presence of Jesus Christ, my weakness, my trials, my struggles, my failures are understood and accepted. *Jesus* knows what you and I go through because Jesus has walked that path before us.

Let me tell you about a field-education supervisor in a seminary. He was a very impressive and prominent big-city preacher. Let's call him "Bill." Bill had an Ivy-league education. He was a nationally certified counselor. A not-very-effective humble, stumbling theological student looked up to him.

One day, while the two of them were alone in Bill's office reviewing some work, Bill suddenly started crying. Right in mid-sentence this big, impressive pastor just burst into tears. His shoulders heaved as he sobbed and sobbed. The student was startled. He put his hand on the supervisor's shoulder to comfort him: role reversal.

After he was done crying, Bill told the student how, in another church, he had gone through a painful divorce. And sometimes the loss and hurt Bill still felt burst through and poured out in tears.

Was Bill less of a pastor because he had known suffering? Was he a less valuable supervisor because he could relate to some of the struggles the student had: the pain and struggle of being untrained and untried and feeling unsure of oneself. Did Bill lose stature in the student's eyes because he could cry?

No. For the student knew Bill could sympathize with his weakness. He knew Bill had been tested, like he had. Bill's tears and his continuing courage in the face of his loss, made him not a smaller but a bigger man to the student.

Jesus, our Great High Priest is always available, always effective, and always understanding. Have you lost a loved one? Jesus wept at the tomb of Lazarus (John 12:35). Are you tempted? Jesus was tempted, too (Mark 1:12ff). Has someone betrayed you? Jesus himself was betrayed and abandoned (Mark 14). Have you been falsely accused? So was he. Have you suffered pain? Jesus was whipped and crucified. Have you had to confront death? Jesus faced death, too. He was tested in every way we are, yet without sinning (Hebrews 15:15).

164

Do Protestants need a priest? *I* think there is one we all need always: one who's praying for us, one who made the ultimate sacrifice for us, one who understands our weaknesses.

Listen to Hebrews: "Since, then, we have a great high priest who has passed through the heavens, Jesus the Son of God ... Let us therefore approach the throne of grace with boldness, so that we may receive mercy and find grace ..." (4:14a, 16, NRSV).

We *have* a Good Priest always. Let's not be afraid to approach him and ask for his help, especially when tempted or tested. Let all the people say, "Amen!"

I Love Luther

Romans 1:8-17

Most of us are familiar with *I Love Lucy*, a sit-com from the late '50s and early '60's — especially those of us who are "forty-something" or older. Remember that famous candy factory episode: Lucy and Ethel trying to keep up with the conveyor belt that moves ever faster and faster? *TV Guide* once ranked that episode the "second-most memorable" moment in television history; second only to Neil Armstrong walking on the moon! That probably says something about memorable moments in television history. *I Love Lucy* is a comedy classic that we can enjoy again and again. Lucille Ball was, up until her death in 1989, America's most beloved redhead.

Many of us could say, "I love Lucy." But how many of us would confess, "I love Luther?" Far fewer, I think. Yet Martin Luther, born in 1483, has undoubtedly had a more lasting effect on all of our lives. It was Martin Luther who, on October 31, 1517, "All Hallows' Eve," nailed 95 theses to the door of the Castle Church at Wittenburg, Germany. These were 95 questions he wanted to debate about the Roman Catholic church's practice of selling indulgences (selling salvation for a price). It was an act of defiance that scholars mark as the beginning of the Protestant Reformation, a church reform movement which swept through Europe and resulted in the development of the Protestant church.

On this Reformation Sunday, let's take a few moments to get reacquainted with Martin Luther. To know Luther is to love many things about him: his faith, his courage, his sincerity, his devotion to Jesus — and the challenge that his example sets for us as Christians today.

One reason I love Luther is for his love of, and commitment to, common people. He didn't always succeed, but he tried very

167

hard to "love his neighbor as he loved himself" (Matthew 22:39). This great hero of the Reformation, who advised princes and kings, and whose writings shook all of Europe, started out painfully poor and never forgot his roots. His father, Hans, was a stern, hardworking miner. When Martin was young, the family was so poor that the boy had to sing for bread in the streets.

Years later, Luther became a doctor of theology, a noted university professor, and a popular preacher and author. But he never lost his deep concern for the spiritual development of common women and men. One of his greatest accomplishments was to translate the entire Bible, all of it, from Hebrew and Greek into German — all by himself. He translated the New Testament, all of it, working day and night, in just eleven weeks. It was a remarkable feat. Luther's translation of the Bible into German is still considered the greatest single influence on the development of the modern German language. But he did it, not for glory, but that men and women could read the Bible in their native tongue. He once published a pamphlet just to answer a question for his barber. The name of the pamphlet was "Master Peter the Barber: a Simple Way to Pray." On other occasions he wrote hymns (over thirty), in order to better reach the common people. Often he wrote his hymns to well-known bar tunes, so they might be more easily learned by people. When criticized for this practice, Luther said, "Why should the devil have all the good tunes?"

Luther was also famous for his down-to-earth illustrations, many of which are too earthy to be included in this sermon! But he was trying to communicate faith in ways the average person could understand. He once said, for instance, that he wished he could learn to pray with the same concentration that his dog — whom he called "Topol" (which means "Blockhead" in German) — had when he stared at a scrap of meat. Ever notice how a dog will stare at you when you're eating, as if willing you to give it something? Luther had noticed that if Blockhead wanted a morsel that Luther held in his hand, he never blinked or took his eyes off it. "Ah," said Luther, "if only we could learn to pray like that!" Luther, like Jesus, saw God in everyday life and drew many of his illustrations from common life.

Also, just like you and me, this brilliant theologian was beset by common emotions. In his case, Luther tended toward depression almost all of his life. He once wrote, "For more than a week, I was close to the gates of hell and death." Another time Luther was so depressed that his wife, Katie, forced him to go outdoors for a walk. When he returned he found Katie dressed all in black, as if for a funeral.

"Who died?" Luther asked.

"God died," replied his good wife, who by the way, was a former nun. "What do you mean, God died?" asked Martin. "You know that's impossible."

"Oh," replied Katie, "I thought God *must have* died, the way *you've* been carrying on!"

Like all of us, Luther could be beset by feelings of discouragement. If only for his common touch, I'm inclined to love this man.

Secondly, I love Luther, and I think you should too, because he had the courage of his convictions. On faith, at the risk of his life, standing on the authority of the Bible, he dared to challenge the most powerful institution of his time, the Roman Catholic church.

In April of 1521, Luther was called to a church council, or "diet" at Worms (Verms) in Germany and commanded to recant, to take back, what he had been writing for the last four years. Luther already knew that other reformers, like John Huss, who had refused to recant, had been condemned and burned at the stake.

Luther was essentially all alone and defenseless, a middle-aged monk in a room crowded with emperors, princes, nobles, bishops, and church lawyers. There was hardly a friendly face in the crowd. Still, with dark eyes flashing and a voice clear and strong, he stood by what he had written, saying, "Unless I am convinced by scripture and plain reason, I do not accept the authority of popes and councils, for they have contradicted each other. My conscience is captive to the Word of God. I cannot and will not recant anything, for to go against conscience is neither safe nor right. God help me, here I stand. Amen."

Of course, God did protect Martin Luther. Powerful supporters kept him safe from his powerful enemies; although he eventually was excommunicated, declared an outlaw and "a wild boar in

169

the vineyard" and an "infamous, blaspheming, heretical scamp." Luther lived the remainder of his adult life with a price on his head.

A second reason for loving Luther was that he had the courage of his convictions. He loved God with all his heart, soul, mind, and strength (see Matthew 22:17).

A third reason I love Luther is for his Christ-centeredness. He once pointed to his heart and said, "If you were to knock on the door of my heart and ask, 'Who lives there?' I would answer 'Jesus Christ.' "

He meant it! For Luther had discovered from painful experience that he couldn't live at peace without Christ in his heart. Luther was *very* pious and very religious. But it was religion driven by fear, not love. Like so many in his time, he lived in terror of an angry, judgmental God. This fear of God's judgment was probably intensified for Luther when he was knocked down by a bolt of lightning in a thunderstorm. He worked very hard to try to please this angry God.

For years, as an Augustinian monk, he tried to live a life of perfection before God. He fasted longer and worked harder than any of the brothers. Often his fellow monks would find Luther on the cold floor of his cell, naked and unconscious after hours of self-denial and prayer. He would confess for hours at a time; so much so that he nearly drove his confessor crazy. Staupitz, his confessor, once said, half-jokingly, "Stop all these petty confessions. Next time see that you have some good, juicy sin to confess, like adultery or murder." But Martin continued to be tortured by feelings of unworthiness and fear.

Until one night, late, preparing for a sermon series on the book of Romans, he read, in a new way, a simple verse, "The one who is righteous by faith will live" (1:17). Suddenly Luther understood that it is our faith in Jesus Christ, in the power of Christ's cross and resurrection, and not our own good works, that makes us "righteous," makes us "right with God," saves us. Luther wrote, "The gates of Paradise opened. I felt I was born again."

Martin Luther had discovered for himself the good news of the gospel. No matter how hard we work, none of us will ever be good enough to save ourselves from our sins. Only God's grace, freely given in the sacrificial death of Jesus, has the power to take away our sins. We are saved by faith alone; which, when we understand it, usually results in loving God and neighbor out of relief, joy, and gratitude. I love Luther because of his Christ-centeredness. He reminded the church, at a critical moment, that salvation comes by faith. And that insight reformed the church.

Common humanity, courage, Christ-centeredness: these are some of the reasons that I love Luther.

One Nation, Under God

Joshua 24:1-3a, 14-25

I pledge allegiance to the flag of the United States of America, and to the Republic for which it stands, one nation, under God, indivisible, with liberty and justice for all.

These are the words of our Pledge of Allegiance. Probably most of us have recited it hundreds of times. But do we know when and why these words were written — and when and how they came to be amended? On this Veterans' Day weekend, when our attention often is focused on things patriotic, I'd like to give you a brief history of the Pledge of Allegiance. As you know, it's been the source of controversy lately. Let's think a bit about what the pledge says, and about what it might mean for America to call itself one nation "under God."

Francis Bellamy wrote the Pledge of Allegiance in August of 1892. He wrote it with a specific occasion in mind. Bellamy created the pledge for Massachusetts schoolchildren to use in a flag raising ceremony on the 400th anniversary of Columbus' landing, on Columbus Day, 1892. His original wording was slightly different. Most significantly, Bellamy did not mention God.

The Pledge of Allegiance was amended to read "one nation, *under God*" by an act of Congress, in 1954, during the Cold War, the Red Scare, and the McCarthy era. Many Americans felt we needed a litmus test to distinguish ourselves from the Soviet Union, which was officially atheistic at the time. The Knights of Columbus led a nationwide campaign to add the words "under God" to the pledge. President Eisenhower signed the legislation after he heard a Presbyterian preacher, The Rev. George Dochety, proclaim that little children in Moscow could easily recite a similar pledge

173

to their hammer-and-sickle flag. About the same time, "In God We Trust" was stamped on all our coins.

Francis Bellamy would likely have objected to the addition. Bellamy, a Baptist minister, had definite Socialist leanings. He had been pressured out of his Boston church for preaching Socialist sermons. Bellamy retired to Florida and eventually stopped attending church altogether because he was offended by the racism he found in Southern churches. His granddaughter said Bellamy would have resented adding "under God" to the pledge. He was interested in bringing people together, said his granddaughter, not dividing them over issues of class, religion, or race.

But most Americans want to keep one nation "under God" in the Pledge of Allegiance. This was clear when a San Francisco appeals court recently ruled the phrase was unconstitutional if used in public schools. According to the ruling, references to God in public schools violate the separation of church and state.

Some folks did not take the issue seriously. A comedian, for example, suggested the pledge would be more accurate if it said, "one nation, under Canada." Another proposed selling commercial space in the Pledge of Allegiance to the highest corporate bidder: "one nation, under Wal-Mart" or "one nation, but 24,000 Starbucks."

The majority of Americans were not amused. According to a *Newsweek* poll, 87 percent of Americans are in favor of keeping the Pledge as it is. Only nine percent would remove the words "under God" from it. The Senate immediately passed an angry resolution, 99 to 0, condemning the appeals court decision. The issue still remains and may eventually be resolved by the Supreme Court.

For now at least, the Pledge of Allegiance proclaims we *are* one nation "under God." But what might that mean? Is it just an empty phrase? Is saying it, as some contend, simply reflexive, like saying "God bless you" when somebody sneezes — a customary saying devoid of real religious meaning? Or should it mean something for Americans to insist on calling ourselves one nation "under God"?

174

Perhaps there's guidance in the Hebrew Scripture passage assigned for this Sunday. A pledge of allegiance is also found in Joshua, chapter 24. Here's the setting: near the end of his life, the aged Joshua calls the people of Israel together at the hill sanctuary at Shechem. He reminds them of the many ways God has acted to save them. Then Joshua challenges the people to choose. Will they publicly pledge allegiance to God? Or will Israel chose to serve other gods?

The people glibly offer God their allegiance: "Um, okay, sure, Joshua, we will serve the Lord, for he is our God. Why not?" Joshua isn't satisfied. He presses them harder. Their promise came too easily, and he won't accept it. Joshua wants Israel to understand how serious this decision is.

He reminds them God is a holy God and a jealous God who won't take second place to anyone. He reminds them God is righteous and judges our sins. A second time the people pledge their allegiance to God. Joshua challenges them again. "You are witnesses against yourselves that you have chosen the Lord, to serve him." "We are witnesses against ourselves," the people proclaim (v. 22 NRSV). Joshua demands they back their pledge up with action: "Then put away your foreign gods and incline your hearts to God."

Three times the people pledge their allegiance to God. Three times Joshua challenges them. One thing I get from Joshua 24 is that it's no empty exercise to proclaim yourselves a nation under God. Pledging allegiance to God is serious business. The exchange in this passage reminds me how serious it is.

God didn't choose the ancient Israelites because they were somehow *better* than other people were. God didn't owe them a thing. All of God's blessings came to Israel as gifts. Couldn't we say the same thing about God's many blessings poured on the United States?

Americans have sometimes thought of *ourselves* as God's "chosen nation." The Plymouth colonists believed they were the New Israel entering the new promised land. The Puritans proclaimed Boston "a city set on a hill," a "beacon" to all nations. If I remember correctly, that's where the name "Beacon Street" came from.

175

Later generations proclaimed it our "manifest destiny," God's plan that the United States should expand all the way to the Pacific. In the Civil War, both Northern and Southern soldiers were utterly convinced they were doing God's will. In fact they often held mass prayer rallies before going to battle to kill each other. Fifty years later doughboys marched off to the First World War proclaiming "God is on our side."

Does God love America? I'd have to say, "Of course." Has God blessed America richly? We'd all agree to that. But does God love America more than all other nations? Is the United States somehow God's chosen people? Are we one nation "under God" because God likes us best?

What do you think? Personally I find an answer to those questions in the words to the hymn, "This Is My Song":

This is my song, O God of all the nations,
a song of peace for lands afar, and mine.
This is my home, the country where my heart is;
here are my hopes, my dreams, my holy shrine....

My country's skies are bluer than the ocean,
and sunlight streams on cloverleaf and pine;
but other lands have sunlight, too, and clover,
and skies are everywhere as blue as mine....
— Lloyd Stone, 1934

This hymn is refreshingly honest and balanced. On the one hand, it celebrates the legitimate love for America that most of us feel. On the other hand it reminds us that other people in other lands have similar feelings for their country. And that other lands are also blessed by God, and God's beloved. The God we worship is the God of all nations, and the God *above* all nations. All nations are "under God," and not just ours.

If we Americans have been chosen for anything, might it be for extra responsibility? At the moment we are the world's only Superpower. We still possess enough weapons of mass destruction to wipe out life on this planet. We are just 6.3 percent of the world's population, but control fifty percent of its wealth. I've read we have a bigger monopoly on the world's grain than the Arabs have on oil. We *could* do a lot to rid the world of hunger. American pop culture has swept around the world. Our multinational corporations have a hand in almost every land. Each of us has an impact on the environment equal to fifteen residents of India.

What would it mean for us really to live as one nation "under God"? In one nation under God, would millions of children go hungry? In one nation under God, would the gap between rich and poor continue to grow? In one nation under God, would toxic waste be dumped on land and sea, extinguishing thousands of species? In one nation under God, would racial injustice continue?

Challenging questions: but the passage from Joshua is a challenging passage. Joshua would not accept a cheap or easy pledge of allegiance. He insisted the Israelites really think about what they were saying. He didn't want them to say, "God is on our side." Rather, he wanted their humble affirmation that, to the best of their ability, as a people, they would try to side with God — two different things.

Abraham Lincoln was not only, to my mind, America's greatest president, but also one of America's great theologians. During the Civil War, Lincoln thought long and hard about what it meant to be one nation "under God." In fact, he used a similar phrase in his Gettysburg Address.

At one point during the Civil War, Lincoln called for a national Day of Prayer and Fasting, rather like Joshua called the people together to recommit themselves to God at Shechem. Like Joshua, Lincoln first recounted God's goodness to the nation. Then he challenged America to live with a renewed faith. This is what Lincoln wrote:

> We have been preserved these many years in peace and prosperity; we have grown in number, wealth and power as no other nation ever has grown. But we have forgotten God. We have forgotten the gracious hand that preserved us in peace and multiplied and enriched and strengthened us; we have vainly imagined, in the deceitfulness of our hearts, that all these things were produced by some superior wisdom and virtue of our

177

own. Intoxicated with unbroken success, we have become too self-sufficient to feel the necessity of redeeming and preserving grace ... Those nations only are blessed whose God is the Lord.

Those nations only are blessed whose God is the Lord. Let me suggest on this day before Veteran's Day that every time we say the Pledge of Allegiance, we renew our commitment to live as "one nation, under God." We don't say "God is on our side," but rather, "We will strive to be on God's side," until that great day comes when there is "liberty and justice for all."

The Greatest Generation

Matthew 11:16-19

"(They) came of age in the Great Depression, when economic despair hovered over the land like a plague ... They answered the call to help save the world from the two most powerful and ruthless military machines ever assembled ... They faced great odds and a late start, but they did not protest."[1] So wrote NBC News anchor Tom Brokaw in his bestseller, *The Greatest Generation*. He was describing the American men and women who helped win the Second World War.

A series of anniversaries, like the sixtieth anniversary of the attack on Pearl Harbor, plus popular movies, like *Saving Private Ryan*, have focused renewed attention to the struggles and sacrifices of "The Builders." Tom Brokaw calls them "The Builders" because they not only won the war, but also built a strong economy, and helped rebuild Western Europe and Japan. They are — many of *you* are — a truly great generation. America is grateful to you. You gave us the prosperous, free country we enjoy today.

On this Sunday before Veteran's Day, let us think a bit on what might make for greatness in *any* generation. For our nation continues to face challenges today. The threats may not be as clear as World War Two. But there remain nagging uncertainties about terrorism. Plus the challenges of poverty, homelessness, violence, and environmental degradation that have plagued us for decades. In 1936, Franklin Delano Roosevelt said, "This generation has a rendezvous with destiny." That was true just before the Second World War. It is equally true today. In each generation America has a "rendezvous with destiny." We might do well to explore what it might take to make us great today.

It seems to me, firstly, that greatness is connected to vision. Let's consider another "Great Generation," the signers of the

179

Declaration of Independence. Those men — John and Samuel Adams, Benjamin Franklin, John Hancock, and Thomas Jefferson among them — *envisioned* a new creation among the world's nations, where all men were created equal and endowed by their Creator with certain inalienable rights.

Admittedly, the rights of life, liberty, and the pursuit of happiness were originally extended only to white, male, property owners. Women and people of color were excluded. It took decades to start to right those wrongs. Still, the signers of the Declaration of Independence had big dreams for America. Their vision for America helped make it great.

What we dream for this country in 2004 is also important. "Where there is no dream, the people perish," Proverbs warns (29:18, KJV). Will we keep dreaming "Patriot dreams" (as in "O beautiful for Patriot dream that sees beyond the years") for America? One dream we need to dream — and work for — is housing for all.

Katharine Lee Bates, author of "America The Beautiful" wrote, "Thine alabaster cities gleam, undimmed by human tears," after her 1904 tour of America's cities. I wonder what Bates would say if she were to visit America's cities today. Few of our present cities are either "alabaster" or "gleaming." Most, including small cities, are "dimmed" by the tears and fears of homeless men and women.

Can we *envision* an America where everyone has adequate food, clothing, and shelter? Can we commit ourselves to working on that problem until it starts to get solved? As Franklin D. Roosevelt put it, "The test of our progress is not whether we add more to the abundance of those who have much; it is whether we provide enough for those have too little."

Another dream we need to dream in 2004 is the dream of a clean environment. Katharine Lee Bates wrote of "spacious skies" and "amber waves of grain ... purple mountain majesties above the fruited plain." That was about 100 years ago. Our skies don't seem quite as "spacious" anymore, when three out of ten Americans breath polluted air, and our plains aren't quite as "fruited" anymore, as farmland is lost at a rate of two million acres a year.

God entrusted us with gift of this magnificent country, "from sea to shining sea." I know sometimes we act like we've forgotten how precious it is. Can we dream of, and work for, a renewed reverence for our environment? It seems to me greatness is tied to vision. Can we envision an America where human needs are met, while the environment is respected?

I think another aspect of greatness is a sense of accountability. Most members of my parents' generation are really good about this. Over and over in Brokaw's book he tells the story of men and women rising up to take responsibility: on the battlefield, on the home front, in business, in their communities, and in raising their children.

Dwight Eisenhower might be a good illustration of accountability in this generation. You perhaps remember the statement Ike made just before D-Day, when the success of the Normandy landings was very much in doubt. As Supreme Allied Commander he wrote, for publication, should the attack fail, "The troops, the Army and the Navy did all that bravery and devotion to duty possibly could. If any blame or fault is attached to this attempt, it is mine alone." What a great statement — greatness tied to a sense of personal accountability! Couldn't we use more accountability like Ike's in America today?

Don't recent corporate scandals seem to call for more responsibility and accountability from some executives and accountants? For example, the accounting firm Arthur Anderson was convicted of obstruction of justice in the Enron scandal. Officials at WorldCom acknowledged that they had hidden 3.8 billion dollars in expenses. Xerox admitted to overstating profits by six billion dollars. Tens of thousands of shareholders and employees got hurt. As President George Bush put it, "Corporate America has got to understand there's a higher calling than trying to fudge the numbers."

We are accountable to each other. One commentator has suggested that we don't just need a Declaration of Independence but also a Declaration of Dependence: the acknowledgment of how much we all depend on each other. We depend on each other to deal honestly and act responsibly for our nation's well-being. We

181

depend on each other to tell the truth, even if, sometimes, the truth hurts. A sense of accountability could well be another aspect of greatness, and another characteristic we need to foster in the United States.

Another critical characteristic of national greatness is the acknowledgment that we depend not only on each other, but also, and ultimately, on God. We do this in our country by putting "God has favored our undertakings" in Latin and "In God we trust" in English on our currency and coins. Another acknowledgment of our dependence on God has been in our Pledge of Allegiance, where we declare ourselves to be "one nation *under God*." This is so widely accepted the earlier District Court ruling came as a shock: the ruling that ordered the removal of "under God." The outcry was so loud around the country that action on that ruling is still being debated.

Our dependence on God has been acknowledged since the early years of our country. Thomas Jefferson was probably the least conventionally religious president that America has ever had. It was Jefferson who rewrote the New Testament. He removed all miracles and all references to the supernatural from it, including Jesus' resurrection.

Even Jefferson strongly acknowledged America's dependence on God. One Sunday morning, during Jefferson's presidency, a friend stopped Jefferson when the president, carrying his prayer book, was on his way to church services. He was going, by the way, to worship on Capitol Hill. I was surprised to learn that regular Sunday services were held in the Capitol, the Treasury Building, the War Department building, and Supreme Court for many years. In fact, the first woman ever officially to speak in the Capitol was a woman preacher who delivered a Sunday sermon there.

Jefferson was on his way to worship at the Capitol when a friend stopped him. "Why are you going to worship?" his friend asked. "You don't believe all the things the preacher says?" Jefferson responded, "No nation has ever yet existed or been governed without religion. Nor can it be." He went on to explain that, as Chief Executive, he was obligated to give religion its proper place.

182

From our founding, America has been "one nation under God." We will continue to be "under God," whether the Pledge of Allegiance ends up saying so or not. I hope it still will. Nevertheless, our nation, and all nations, rely on God's providence and stand under God's judgment. Abraham Lincoln's warning, written in 1863, is still pertinent today. Lincoln wrote, in the midst of the Civil War:

> *We have grown in numbers, wealth and power as no other nation ever has grown. But we have forgotten God. We have forgotten the gracious hand that preserves us in peace, and multiplied and enriched and strengthened us; as we have vainly imagined ... that all these blessings were produced by some superior wisdom and virtue of our own. Intoxicated with unbroken success we have become too self-sufficient to feel the necessity of redeeming and preserving grace; too proud to pray to the God who made us.*

May that not be so for us. Rather may we acknowledge, now and always, our dependence on God.

I read somewhere that Tom Brokaw ran into a young fireman at Ground Zero in New York City after September 11. The fireman was part of the rescue efforts after the collapse of the Twin Towers. In a clear reference to Brokaw's book, the young fireman said something like, "Just watch us now, Mr. Brokaw, and see if this generation has what it takes for greatness." To me, greatness includes concern for the least among us, respect for the land God has entrusted to us, accountability to each other, and acknowledgment of our dependence on God. In the scripture lesson I read this morning, Jesus asks, "... to what will I compare this generation?" We might all compare ourselves to those standards and see if, in our time, as Jesus puts it, "... wisdom is vindicated by her deeds" (Matthew 11:16a, 19b NRSV).

---

1. Tom Brokaw, *The Greatest Generation* (New York: Randon House, 1998), p. xix.

183

Don't Be A Turkey!

Luke 17:11-19

There is little question that the commercially grown turkey is, pound for pound, one of nature's less intelligent creatures, at least according to an article I once read. In that article, author Fred McGuiness calls the domesticated turkey "as brainless as a baseball," and describes how turkeys can have trouble doing even simple things.

For example, your average turkey can get into trouble doing something as simple as eating. Turkeys have been known to starve to death right next to a mountain of food. But other times they will eat so much so quickly that grain will fill their gullets and they die by choking. Drinking water can be a problem for turkeys, too. Farmers frequently find them drowned in shallow troughs. If a turkey is outdoors, looking up at the sky when it starts to rain, and it's mouth is open, it can die. They're often not smart enough to close their mouths in the rain, and so they can drown standing up. Eating and drinking can put a strain on turkey intelligence. No wonder, a few years back, when teenagers wanted to insult each other, they would call each other a "Turkey."

But at least the turkey has an excuse for being "bird-brained." It has a bird's brain! There is less excuse for human beings. Take the nine lepers Luke writes about in the lesson I read. Didn't that group include some pretty big turkeys?! Jesus had given them a tremendous, free gift. He had healed all ten from a disgusting, painful, and unsightly skin disease. Even more important, he had made it possible for them to re-enter society and to be reunited with their families. Ten lepers were healed. But only one leper, and a Samaritan at that, came back and said "Thanks."

There are relatively few things in the gospel accounts that actually surprise Jesus. In most situations, he seems to know what's

185

going to happen before it occurs. But in this case, even Jesus registers surprise. "Were not ten healed?" he asks incredulously. "Where are the other nine?" Jesus was astonished by their ingratitude. Ten received God's blessing, but only one in ten stopped to say thanks.

What about us? Thanksgiving Day is approaching, and among which group will we be found? Among the nine who forget? Or with the one who came back to thank God?

No one wants to be a turkey. If *we* want to avoid being "turkeys" this Thanksgiving, the behavior of that tenth leper in Luke's lesson might prove instructive. What was there about this one man that set him apart? First, it says in verse 15 that when the man *saw* that he was healed, he came back and gave thanks. So, a first step in thanks-giving is perceiving, *seeing* the ways we've been blessed.

God has given different creatures different ways of seeing. I once read that a hawk, perched on top of the Empire State building, could locate a dime on the sidewalk below. Of course, I don't know why a hawk would *care* about a dime located on the sidewalk below the Empire State Building! But, if a dime were there, the hawk could spot it. The hawk's vision is eight times more acute than ours.

A bee has a different kind of vision. Its eyes have 15,000 facets that enable it to see the sun as a single dot and to navigate long distances with the sun as a reference. A kingfisher has two kinds of vision: one for spotting fish as it flies overhead and another for seeing fish underwater.

There are different ways of seeing, and we may need to see things in different ways if we are to experience the full measure of our blessings. Of course, some of our blessings ought to be easy to see. Maybe some of us here this morning, like the leper in the story, have been healed from a terrible illness. Maybe there have been other dramatic good things that have happened for us or for our family in the past year. All of us here this morning are profoundly lucky to be living where we are: in America and not in Bosnia or Iraq or the Gaza Strip or some other troubled location. We're all blessed that we have plenty to eat: sometimes maybe even too much. We are blessed that we can go home to warm,

186

comfortable houses or apartments and don't have to sleep in a shelter or on a heating grate in the sidewalk of some city street. Some of our blessings ought to be completely obvious.

Maybe other blessings require another kind of "seeing" because they're more subtle. Can we thank God this Thanksgiving not only for the good things that happened, but also for the bad things that didn't happen? The problems and disasters we worried about which did not come about?

Can we look in a different way still and see some sort of blessing even in the problems that we do face? As George Matheson, the beloved Scottish preacher once put it, "I've thanked God a thousand times for my 'roses.' Now I've got to learn to thank God for my 'thorns.'" George Matheson happened to be blind — which is a pretty significant "thorn."

In the end, Matheson was able to see, with his spiritual eye, some "hidden" blessings in his blindness. He found his lack of sight forced him to become a better listener, to be more patient with others, to be more willing to receive the help and care of others, to be more sensitive to other people's suffering. It also helped Matheson identify with the Apostle Paul, who had his own "thorn in the flesh." Most importantly, it helped Matheson better to appreciate the sufferings and sacrifices of Jesus, who not only had a thorn, but who wore a crown of thorns.

A first step in the tenth leper's journey to thanks-giving was simply *seeing*. Maybe, if we think about it a bit, we can find different ways of seeing our blessings, too.

We notice, secondly, that this leper went beyond just *seeing* to *saying*. Luke writes, continuing on in verse 15, "When he (the leper) saw that he was healed, (he) turned back, praising God with a loud voice." The leper's thanks-giving began with perception but then moved to proclamation. He took time to actually say "thank you" to God.

There's an old proverb that goes, "The thankful person tastes his joy twice." She or he tastes it when it happens and tastes it again in speaking about it. If we go to an art gallery and view a beautiful work of art, or go to the movies and watch a movie that

187

really moves us, part of the joy and wonder of those experiences is expressing our gratitude and appreciation for the gifts of the artist.

We're not meant to keep gratitude and appreciation bottled up inside! This Thanksgiving, if we have things to be thankful about, we need to *say* our thanks to God!

Let me suggest some practical applications for this Thanksgiving. Make plans in your household to say "thank you" to God. You may want to write down what you're thankful for on a slip of paper. You may want to share your thanks, round-robin fashion, around the Thanksgiving table. Perhaps the children could be asked to draw a picture of what they're grateful for this Thanksgiving, and share it. Maybe your family could join in a Thanksgiving hymn or in a brief Thanksgiving service, like we will be using at our church dinners this evening. Perhaps you might want to look for and raise up some of the wonderful Psalms of thanks-giving. To properly thank God, we must not only see what we're thankful for but also to say it. That's the second lesson we learn from the leper who returned.

The third lesson is not in scripture. But it is in tradition. Tradition has it that this tenth leper was the one who spread the good news about Jesus Christ throughout Samaria. Tradition has it that he, a healed leper, paid particular attention to telling other lepers how Jesus had made him whole. Is it true? I don't know. It's a tradition. But he also *shared.*

"Thanks," after all, is only half of the word "Thanksgiving." "Giving" is the other half of the word. Herbert Hoover was not the most notable or quotable of our American presidents. But he did say, "Give for the joy of giving, and sing hymns of thankfulness that you have (something) to give."

We are all very fortunate to have something to give. In the West Virginia hills they have a custom of setting an extra place setting and an extra chair at the Thanksgiving table. It's a reminder that there will always be people in need — and we need to make room in our hearts and in our giving for people in need.

Leonard Sweet, writing in *Homiletics* magazine, has some perceptive things to say about the holiday that is before us. He writes:

188

(Thanksgiving) itself is becoming a kind of great divide separating ... the "haves" from the "have nots." For the ..."haves," Thanksgiving is the starting gun for the first frenetic round of holiday shopping. Isn't this the biggest shopping day with the biggest sales in your community? Those who "have" even more may use this long weekend as time for the first skiing vacation of the winter ... with enough time and enough money (you) can find snow somewhere.

For the "have nots," Thanksgiving marks a new beginning as well. In the "have not" culture, Thanksgiving is the first disappointment of the ... holiday season. For the lucky ones, it's a ... meal served cafeteria-style at a church or mission. The food is nourishing, the spirit welcoming. But it is surely not the Thanksgiving of anyone's dreams.

One of the most disappointing things about the "have not" Thanksgiving is there are no leftovers ... no leftover goodies ... no leftover family members to spend the long weekend with ... no leftover feelings of security ...[1]

I suspect all of us here this morning are fortunate enough to be among the "haves." Will we make generous giving a part of our thanks-giving? Remember, every time we feed the hungry, give drink to the thirsty, clothe the naked, visit the sick or the prisoner, it's the same thing as doing it for Jesus (see Matthew 25:31-46). The tenth leper may not have had much. But, according to tradition, in his gratitude, he shared what he had to give.

This Thanksgiving, don't be a turkey. In English, the word "think" and the word "thank" both come from the same root. Nine out of ten forgot to think and forgot to thank God for their blessings. But the tenth leper *saw* his blessings, *said* thanks for his blessings and *shared* his blessings. And so can we.

---

1. Leonard Sweet, writing in *Homiletics* magazine (Canton, Ohio: Communications Resources, Inc., October-December, 1996). p 34, used by permission.

To Be A Pilgrim

Hebrews 11:1-3, 13-16

What do you think of when you hear the word "Pilgrim"? Most of us — especially around Thanksgiving — hear the word "Pilgrim" and think of the English Separatists who crossed the Atlantic on the *Mayflower*, landed on Cape Cod, and settled in Plymouth. We hear "Pilgrim" and think "Thanksgiving."

But, when you think of *that kind* of Pilgrim, what do you think? Some consider the Pilgrims stained-glass saints. A church in Utica, New York, was designed as a shrine to the Pilgrims. Three tall stained-glass windows behind the altar, the center of worship, depict the Pilgrims landing at Plymouth Rock. Another entire wall is covered with magnificent Tiffany windows, thirty feet high. They portray William Brewster delivering the first sermon in New England. His kneeling congregation is dressed somberly in gray and brown. Several men stand guard with muskets. Or maybe they are on the lookout for turkeys. At the top, Tiffany angels smile approvingly from heaven.

Nowhere in that huge sanctuary (it seats 600) *nowhere* was there a picture of Jesus! Nowhere! Plymouth Congregational Church seemed to have been built to beatify the Pilgrims! Some folks *do* revere the Pilgrims like that.

Others depict them more darkly. Most of the *Mayflower* Pilgrims were Puritans, and "Puritanical" is not a happy word. Some depict the Puritans as severe, austere, rigid, religious fanatics. Historian George Willison writes, they were "fond of controversy, and sharp of tongue, engaging in many a high-pitched quarrel with friends and foes alike...." H. L. Mencken defines Puritanism as "the haunting fear that someone, somewhere, may be happy."

But they weren't sullen and sour. They wore bright clothing. They loved to listen to music: just *not* in *church*. The Pilgrims

191

thought the organ was the "voice of the devil." They found choirs "distracting."

Still, they weren't monks or nuns. They married early, often, and late; and produced lots of children. They loved to drink — especially beer. That's what they used their pumpkins for, by the way, not pumpkin pies. The Pilgrims mixed pumpkins, parsnips, and walnut chips and brewed pumpkin beer. I don't think that's going to catch on in any microbrewery anytime soon!

The Pilgrims were neither rigid fanatics nor stained-glass saints. They were ordinary people with extraordinary faith. They were, like most of us, on a pilgrimage, searching for truth and a closer connection to God. Let's take a few moments to think about what it means "to be a Pilgrim," both in the 1620s and today.

To be a Pilgrim means having the courage to act on your commitments. The *Mayflower* Pilgrims' courage was clear when they left Holland. This little band, described by William Bradford as "seventy menfolk and women, 32 good children, a handful of cocks and hens, and two dogs" had no illusions about the dangers that lay ahead of them.

In his historical book, *Of Plymouth Plantation*, Bradford discloses the colonists' worst fears. They expected "famine, nakedness, continual danger from the savage people, who are cruel, barbarous, and most treacherous, being most ferocious in their rage and merciless when they overcome."

Their chances for survival seemed slim. It was too late in the year for an easy Atlantic crossing, and too late to plant crops. They had scanty supplies. The men knew little about hunting or fishing — and less about fighting. Still, as one of their spokesmen put it, "It is not with us as with other men, whom small things discourage."[1] The Pilgrims had the courage to go forward, no matter what it might cost.

It took even greater courage to stay in Plymouth after they landed. During the first winter, conditions were worse than they imagined. There were great gray wolves, whose howls terrorized the colonists at night. There was "The Great Sickness." Over half the Pilgrims died. They buried their dead at night in unmarked graves so the Native Americans wouldn't know how weak they

192

were getting. At one time only seven Pilgrims were well enough to tend the sick.

Yet, in spite of that terrible winter, none of the survivors returned to England on the *Mayflower* in the spring, when they had the opportunity. As the *Mayflower* sailed over the horizon, the Pilgrims stood on the shore and wept. Few expected to live until the ship returned.

The Pilgrims had the courage to act on their commitments, no matter what. Do we?

Sociologist Robert Bellah, author of *Habits of the Heart*, is impressed by the power of religion. He once said, "We should not underestimate the significance of the small group of people who have a new vision of a just and gentle world. The quality of a culture may be changed when two percent of its people have a new vision (and act on it)."[2]

Christians make up far more than two percent of our town, far more than two percent of Massachusetts, far more than two percent of Americans. So, why don't we have a greater effect: on issues of the environment, on justice for the needy, on the quality of life on Cape Cod? Could it be we need more courage to act on our commitments? To be a Pilgrim means to stand up for what you believe, no matter what.

To be a Pilgrim also means sharing what you have, and turning thanks into giving. The Pilgrim colonists willingly shared all they had. During their first three years, all property was held in common. At one point, they were down to five kernels of corn per day for food. Still, they divided the corn kernels up equally. And, the original group of fifty that survived the first winter shared their limited food with the sixty newcomers who arrived in the spring.

One of their finest moments came in 1623, at the first real Thanksgiving. The small colony hosted over ninety Native American braves for three days. There was eating and drinking, wrestling, footraces, and gun and arrow-shooting competitions. It was the Pilgrims' way of saying "Thank you" to God, and to the Native Americans who had helped them survive. To be a Pilgrim means sharing and turning thanks into giving. How thankful and giving are we?

193

We have a lot to be thankful for — much more than the Pilgrims — don't we? They originally rejected Cape Cod as unsuitable for living. Today the Cape is the seventh most popular retirement location in America, and the fastest growing region in the state. The Pilgrims so suffered from inadequate health care that half of them died. Today their local hospital is one of America's 100 best. The Pilgrims depended on their fall harvest for survival. Today, many depend on stocks and bonds.

We have *much* to be thankful for. But we could do more. The World Bank has estimated that if only *two percent* of the world's food — only *two percent* of the world's food — was diverted from wealthy nations (like ours) to poor nations, *everyone* on the planet would have an adequate diet! Isn't that incredible: a two-percent shift in foods would wipe out world hunger! Most of us waste more than two percent of our food every day.

If we could change, and encourage our government to change, maybe 33,000 children a day wouldn't die from hunger. Maybe there wouldn't be four and one-half million homeless people on America's streets. Maybe 30,000,000 Americans wouldn't be malnourished.

To be a Pilgrim is to share and to turn thanks into giving, recognizing what God has already given us.

Finally, to be a Pilgrim is to travel hopefully toward the future, trusting God to fulfill God's promises. The Plymouth colonists saw themselves on a pilgrimage. Like the heroes of faith listed in the eleventh chapter of Hebrews, they knew they were "strangers and foreigners on ... earth ... seeking a homeland" assured by God (11:13-14). The Pilgrims were not prisoners of the past. They looked forward with hope to the future, believing that, through God's goodness, the best was yet to come.

They gave up the familiarity of England, for Holland, because the English church resisted reformation. They left comfortable Holland for the New World because their children were assimilating to Dutch ways. They sought a homeland in what Cotton Mather called "this howling wilderness" of New England, believing that God would fulfill God's promises, and somehow use their pain and suffering to produce good. They believed, as William Bradford

194

put it, "Their condition was not ordinary, their ends were good and honorable, their calling lawful and urgent" and therefore they would receive "the blessings of God." Which they did.

The Pilgrims traveled hopefully, with faith in the future. Do we? Do we believe that if we work and struggle and sacrifice, this church can be even better than it is already (and it's pretty darned good)? Do we believe that we, as individuals, are heading for a Homeland, too: a glorious homeland we cannot earn, but can only receive through faith? There is power when we live, not tied to the past, but as "strangers and foreigners" passing through life as Pilgrims, looking forward to, and struggling for, the homeland God has promised.

To be a Pilgrim is to have the courage of our convictions, to turn thanks into giving, and to cling to God's promise that the best is yet ahead of us.

There's power in that kind of Pilgrim faith. Power to build a new society. With that kind of faith, I wonder, what might you and I do?

---

1. William Bradford, *Of Plymouth Plantation: The Pilgrims In America*, edited by Harvey Wish (New York: Capricorn Books, 1962).

2. John R. W. Stott (quoting Robert Bellah), "Christians, Salt, And Light" (*Preaching Today* Audio Series, Tape No. 109, 1992).

Don't Forget The Child!

Micah 5:2-5a; Luke 1:46-55

Most of us are familiar with the blockbuster movies, *Home Alone* and *Lost in New York: Home Alone 2*. In *Home Alone*, little nine-year-old Kevin is accidentally left behind in the Chicago suburbs while his family flies off for a Christmas vacation in Paris. In its sequel, Kevin mistakenly boards a plane for New York City while the rest of his family heads off to Florida.

Several recent real-life cases of child neglect have made the concept of leaving young children home alone a whole lot less funny. Does anyone remember the Chicago couple who left *their* nine-year-old to take care of herself *and* her four-year-old sister, while they went off on vacation for nine days to Mexico?

The movies should have contained a scene where Kevin's parents had to explain a few things to a judge: explain why *they're* not guilty of child neglect! They seem like nice people. They take great vacations. But especially around Christmas, you *don't forget the child!*

But then, if we're honest with ourselves, we might have to admit that sometimes we can be guilty of "child neglecting," around Christmas. Not neglecting our own children or grandchildren, of course. They have their ways of not letting us forget them, especially around Christmas!

No, the child we sometimes "ignore," "overlook," "leave behind," or "neglect" is God's Son. For many of us, this Christmas season, and especially this last week of Advent, is a frightfully busy time: the biggest shopping days of the year, one of the busiest travel periods of the year, a time when many businesses hope to make, often *need* to make up to 45 percent of their annual profits. For many, it's a time of mounting celebrations and office parties, a time of writing out cards, wrapping gifts, hanging lights, decorating trees, and baking brownies. Sometimes we get so absorbed in preparing for Christmas that we forget the reason for the season. One of our church members puts it well. In the midst of all the frantic activity in this season, our Christmas can become "Xmas," with the Christ "X-ed" out.

It's often been easy to overlook the Child. He was, after all, largely ignored, overlooked, and neglected by the world on that first Christmas. "He was in the world, and the world was made through him, yet the world knew him not. He came to his own home, and his own people received him not" (John 1:10-11 RSV). You see, during the period when Christ was born, the world's attention was focused, not on Bethlehem, but on Rome.

"All roads lead to Rome." Rome was where everything important was happening. The Roman Empire was the greatest political and economic creation of the Ancient World. It was huge, stretching from the Atlantic Ocean on the west, to the Euphrates on the east. It stretched, at that time, as far south as the Sahara Desert and as far north as the Danube. And all this massive empire was ruled by one man. Caesar Augustus was his name.

Tucked away in Caesar's mighty empire was a narrow strip of land along the Mediterranean known as Palestine; an impoverished, conquered territory that was considered a cultural backwater. Tucked into one corner of Palestine near the south, in a hilly region, was the little town of Bethlehem. Its name in Hebrew means "House of Bread." It was a village as plain and ordinary as a loaf of bread.

If someone had told Caesar Augustus, sitting in his palace in the capital, Rome, that history was about to be made by a Jewish baby, being born in Bethlehem, into a family headed by a hillbilly father, born to a teenage mother, he would have laughed. Caesar would not have known where Bethlehem was. It was too insignificant a spot to attract the attention of someone like him. Besides, Caesar would have contended that history is made, not by weak, defenseless babies, but by people like him. After all, hadn't he just ordered a census so that "all the world should be enrolled" (Luke 2:1 RSV) that was disrupting the entire world? Even if he had known about the birth of Jesus, Caesar Augustus, in his pomp and circumstance, would have considered it of no account. Caesar Augustus was among those who overlooked the child.

Most of the people of his time ignored him. We may sometimes forget him. But God does not forget Jesus! Eight hundred years before Caesar Augustus, Micah, God's prophet, informed the world about how it would go. Micah spoke these words in the name of the Lord:

Bethlehem... you are one of the smallest towns in Judah, but out of you will I bring a Ruler for Israel, whose family line goes back to ancient times. When he comes, he will rule his people with the strength that comes from the Lord and with the majesty of the Lord God himself. His people will live in safety because people all over the earth will acknowledge his greatness, and he will bring peace. — Micah 5:2-5a (TEV)

Eight long centuries *before* Christ, the Lord God put his finger on little Bethlehem, the insignificant "House of Bread," and announced that this backwater village would be the birthplace of his Son. Caesar Augustus no doubt thought *he* was pretty clever ordering that census. But mighty Caesar was only a messenger boy, a minor character in the plot. Caesar, and the whole machinery of the Roman Empire were merely God's instruments to get Mary and Joseph to travel from Nazareth to Bethlehem, a distance of eighty miles. God had a plan. God had never forgotten the Child!

You see, it's often what we consider insignificant that God considers important. It is what we consider important that God considers insignificant. An impoverished land, a backwater village, a run-down stable, a teenage mother, a poor child's birth: we might overlook them. A mighty Caesar, an enormous palace, prestige and power: we might be impressed. But God's values are often the reverse of this world's.

Mary, the mother of Jesus, was a woman who was humble, plain, and simple, but also obedient, insightful, and faithful. With her simple faith, Mary understood a lot of the values of God. Mary

199

praised God's ways in the "Magnificat," a hymn that the early church attributed to her:

> *(God) has shown strength with his arm, he has scattered the proud (like Caesar Augustus) in the imagination of their hearts, he has put down the mighty from their thrones, and exalted those (like Mary) of low degree; he has filled the hungry with good things, and the rich he has sent empty away.*
> — Luke 1:51-53 (RSV)

Christmas is more than just a family holiday; more than just a winter-time celebration to "knock back" the dark and the cold; more than just an economic and social event; more than just an opportunity to play host to co-workers, neighbors, and friends (although it *is* all of these things, too!). It is the breaking into our world of God's long-awaited Messiah. It is God's overturning of the values of our world. It is the promise that, through this Child, this Christ, the *spiritually* hungry *and* the *physically* hungry *will be* fed. It is the miracle of the Incarnation, God becoming flesh and dwelling among us. It is the beginning of the ultimate act of love: God wanting so much to communicate with us, to share God's self with us, that God breaks into our world and becomes a human being. A human being who willingly dies for us on a cross! It's the Light of God shining in our world's darkness, and overcoming the darkness.

You don't see all this if you only look at the birth of Christ with the eyes of Caesar, with the jaded eyes of the world. You have to look at Christmas with the eyes of Mary, the eyes of wondering faith.

I really hope you enjoy this Christmas! Go out and celebrate! Laugh and exchange gifts and eat too much; rejoice in life, thank God for family and friends, squeeze your grandchildren until they think they'll burst! Like any loving Parent, God is happy when God's children are happy. God rejoices in our holiday joy.

But don't forget, Christmas is not just something passing. It's something radical. It's the bursting of God into our world. It's the overturning of the values of this world. It's the fulfillment of prophesy and God's plan which has unfolded since the beginning of creation. Let it be a time of awe and reverence and wonderment, of inviting the Child into your heart.

Do it all! Really celebrate Christmas! We need that light in the darkness. But in the midst of it all, don't forget the Child!

A Christmas That Lasts

Luke 2:1-20

I would imagine that any one of us here this morning could tell an amusing story or two about unusual items that they have received at Christmas. At one time or another, most adults have gotten gifts that they consider just a little bit odd: like a battery-operated tie that flashes in the dark, or a water-proofed radio to play in the shower, or a year's supply of Norwegian sardines.

One such gift came in a Christmas card. When it was opened, along with the card, a packet fell out. On one side it read: "Sprouts Birth of Jesus. Drop capsules in warm water and watch!" On the other side it continued, "Fun, educational, non-toxic, for children five years old and older. Not to be taken internally. Each capsule contains a different figure: Mary, Joseph, Baby Jesus, Creche ... Cross Publishing Company. Made in the USA."

What we had was a clear plastic wrapper containing four pill-sized capsules. When you placed the capsules in warm water, they dissolved and four sponge figurines, which have been packed tightly into the capsules, break out. Here's Mary, Joseph, the Creche, and the Baby Jesus. Christmas in a capsule. What will they think of next?!

The little toy provided a moment of amusement and diversion, but when you come right down to it, it's kind of lightweight, disposable, easily lost, discarded, or forgotten. It treats the Nativity as a novelty and little more.

Sadly, some folks will experience a Christmas that has little more substance or permanence than one of those sponge-rubber figures. A Christmas equally capsulized. A Christmas not taken internally. A Christmas that is a mere novelty and little more.

In just a few days, once the scraps of wrapping paper are finally picked up off the living room floor, the leftovers are eaten, the guests have gone home, and the tree is taken down, then, for some folks, Christmas will be over until next December. Nothing will be left of Christmas — except the unpaid bills!

I think that's a shame! On the other hand, I believe it is possible to have a lasting Christmas, a Christmas that means as much to us in July as it means right now. One component of a Christmas that lasts is a continuing sense of wonder: the miracle of Almighty Good emptying God's self, taking the form of a servant, coming down to earth as a helpless infant, born in the likeness of human beings; the sudden appearance of the angelic chorus to the astonished shepherds out in the fields, the marvelous journey of the three kings to lay their treasures at the feet of an unknown peasant child in a dirty cattle stall. When we think about the elements of the Nativity story, we find, with Mary, that there is much to "ponder in our hearts." Christmas ought to give us "a rebirth of wonder."

But that sense of wonder and surprise need not be confined to Christmas. For the mysteries of God are there to be savored all of the year. There was an entomologist, a scientist who studies insects, who had spent his entire career studying a certain type of beetle. Turns out he was one of the world's foremost authorities on this particular beetle.

For decades, this scientist had devoted his life to the study of this insect, capturing it in the woods, breeding it in the laboratory, putting them under a microscope, publishing papers about them.

After much thought, one realizes that this man had a really healthy perspective. He was a Christian. And it was his belief that in finding out as much as he could about this particular beetle, he was helping to bring glory to God. God, after all, was the one who had fashioned these insects. The scientist wrote that even after a lifetime of study, he felt he had barely scratched the surface in understanding his subject. He was still amazed as to how complex this insect was. It remained a marvel and a mystery to him.

Another scientist, Albert Einstein, once wrote: "The most beautiful thing we can experience is the mysterious. It is the source of all true art and science. He to whom this emotion is a stranger, who can no longer pause to wonder, and stand wrapped in awe is as good as dead; his eyes are closed."

204

The Creator's wonders are all around us: from the tiniest insect to the vast reaches of the heavens and ocean, to a fragile flake of snow. All we need to do is open our eyes! The mysteries of Christ's birth remind us that life is bigger than our precise calculations and neat explanations. A continuing sense of wonder is a component of a Christmas that lasts.

So also is a lively belief in the existence of things spiritual. Christmas also is about the breaking into our world of a largely unseen world, the world of the spirit. It reminds us that there are truths beyond the truths we take for granted. As we ponder the Nativity story, it ought to have the effect of enlarging the horizons of our minds.

Take the existence of angels, for example. During Christmas, we hear about angels, we sing about angels, we hang angels on our trees. But then we tend to put them aside for another year. But the scriptures speak, nearly 100 times, about the existence of angels. They are portrayed as God's messengers and our personal helpers. The Nativity reminds us of spiritual possibilities beyond our everyday world. I don't know whether you believe in angels or not. Many Americans do ... about 65 percent.

Angels are a "hot" topic right now. Could you at least consider the possibility that angels exist? There's a lot of anecdotal evidence that they do ...

Time magazine had a story of an angelic encounter, told by a woman named Ann Cannady.

Cannady is the second wife of a retired Air Force Master Sargeant named Gary who had lost his first wife to cancer. It turned out, after some years of marriage, that Ann Cannady was diagnosed as having advanced cancer herself. Of course, both she and her husband were crushed. They spent the weeks before a pending operation for her scared and praying. Ann prayed, "Please (God), if I'm going to die, let me die quickly. I don't want Gary to have to face this again."

Ann is convinced her prayers were answered. One morning, three days before she was to enter the hospital for surgery, Gary answered the door. Standing on the step was a large man, a good inch taller than her six-foot-five-inch husband. "He was the blackest

205

black I'd ever seen," says Ann, "and his eyes were a deep, deep azure blue." The stranger introduced himself simply as Thomas. Then he told her that her cancer was gone.

Ann, still confused, looked at the man and demanded, "Who are you?"

He responded, "I am Thomas. I am sent by God."

Next, Ann recalls, "He held up his right hand, palm facing me, and leaned toward me, though he didn't touch me." The heat coming out of his hand, she reports, was incredible. Suddenly she felt her legs go out from under her and she fell to the floor. As she lay there, a strong white light, like a searchlight, traveled through her body. When she awoke, Thomas was gone and her husband was standing over her, asking her if she were still alive and begging her to speak.

Ann was convinced that Thomas was an angel visitor and that she had been healed. Her doctor was skeptical and put it down as stress. Still, at her insistence, he conducted a biopsy before subjecting her to the operation. The doctor discovered, much to his amazement, that the cancer was completely gone. It has not returned for fifteen years![1]

There are lots of stories about the existence of angels. To me, Ann's story, and others like it, reinforce the idea that the biblical account of angelic visitors is literally true. That's *my* opinion. You might share it, or not. But Christmas reminds us that there *are* truths beyond the truth that we take for granted. Who knows when one of God's angels might appear — maybe even to you!

Too often we experience a disposable, throw-away Christmas; a Christmas with about as much substance as one of these toys. But *I* contend that Christmas is not meant to be packed away, capsulized into one month, or maybe five weeks, and then *forgotten*. Christmas is meant to give us a new perspective on life. When we look at the things of this world with a renewed sense of wonder; when we have a lively belief in things spiritual, we bring something of Christmas into our daily living. We break Christmas out of its capsule and begin to experience a *Christmas* that *lasts*.

1. Nancy Gibbs, "Angels Among Us," *Time* magazine (New York: Time, Inc., December 27, 1992), pp. 59-60, the story of Ann Cannady.